THE THWARTING OF BARON BOLLIGREW

CHARACTERS
(in order of their appearance)

STORYTELLER
THE DUKE
HIS KNIGHTS
SIR DIGBY VAYNE-TRUMPINGTON
SIR GRACELESS STRONGBODY
SIR PERCIVAL SMOOTHELY-SMOOTHE
SIR OBLONG fitz OBLONG
JUNIPER
CAPTAIN
JASPER, 15TH BARON BOLLIGREW
SQUIRE BLACKHEART
PEASANTS
MEN-AT-ARMS
LORD MAYOR
OBIDIAH, a peasant
MAGPIE
A SECRETARY
DR MOLOCH
MAZEPPA
THE DRAGON
A CORPORAL
A COOK
DRUMMER AND CYMBALIST

The action of the play
takes place on a bare stage

THE THWARTING OF BARON BOLLIGREW

A Comedy

by

ROBERT BOLT

SAMUEL FRENCH

LONDON
NEW YORK SYDNEY TORONTO HOLLYWOOD

ISBN 0 573 0 5020 1

PRINTED IN GREAT BRITAIN BY
W. & J. MACKAY & CO LTD, CHATHAM

ACT I

The CURTAIN *rises on a stage which is dark except for a single spot down* c, *in which stands the* STORYTELLER. *He wears something unique, to set him apart.*

STORYTELLER. A long time ago—in the days when dragons were still common—there lived a Duke. And whenever news was brought in of a dragon ravaging some part of the country the Duke sent one of his Knights away in shining armour to deal with it. After a few weeks the Knight would return with the tip of the dragon's tail to prove that he had killed it. Dragons are excessively vain, and when the tips of their tails are cut off they die, of mulligrubs. The return of the Knights would be announced like this:

(*A fanfare sounds. The* LIGHTS *come up, revealing a stage bare of scenery except for drapes and a cyclorama. At a round table sit the* DUKE *and the* KNIGHTS. *The* DUKE *is an elderly, well-fed aristocrat, well-meaning and indolent. He wears civilian garb, fairy-tale period. The* KNIGHTS *wear armour, except for* JUNIPER, *who wears less magnificent civvies than the Duke. They wear surcoats bearing the Royal Shawberry. The seat on Duke's* L *is vacant, and other empty ones are to be seen round the table*)

(*Moving to one side and announcing*) Sir Digby Vayne-Trumpington!

(TRUMPINGTON *enters*)

DUKE. Ah, there you are, Trumpington. Glad to have you back. Got the tip of the dragon's tail?

(TRUMPINGTON *places the bright blue tail-tip on the table. The* DUKE *inspects it*)

Not very big, is it?

TRUMPINGTON. It was not a large dragon, Your Grace, no; but singularly vicious.

FIRST KNIGHT. They can be tricky, those little blue beggars.

(*There is a murmur of agreement*)

DUKE. Not complaining, Trumpington. We can't all be St Georges, can we?

(*While* TRUMPINGTON *sits, there is a fanfare*)

STORYTELLER. Sir Graceless Strongbody!

(*There is a pause all looking off expectantly*)

DUKE (*indulgently*) Likes to make an entrance, Strongbody . . .
(*The pause continues. Less indulgently*) Call him again.
STORYTELLER. Sir Grace . . . !

(STRONGBODY *enters dragging a huge green tail. Murmurs of appreciation and then polite clapping come from the* KNIGHTS)

DUKE. I must *say*, Graceless! I think we'll have this stuffed,
gentlemen. How d'you do it?
STRONGBODY (*gruffly*) Oh, usual methods, ye know.
DUKE. Aha—"Deeds not Words", the old Strongbody motto.

(*There is another fanfare*)

STORYTELLER. Sir Percival Smoothely-Smoothe!

(SMOOTHE *enters*)

DUKE. Good show, Smoothe; back on time as usual. Find your
dragon?

(SMOOTHE *puts down two red tail-tips*)

Good Lord, *two* dragons!
SMOOTHE. No, Your Grace, one dragon with two tails.
DUKE. Well I never saw such a thing in my life. Gave you a bit of
trouble I dare say?
SMOOTHE (*sitting*) Not really, Your Grace. It seemed to be con-
fused.
DUKE. Ah, modest, modest. I like that, Smoothe, like it. Well
now, who's missing? (*Looking at the vacant seat to his* L) Oh, Oblong.
Not like him to be late. Well we'll just wait for Oblong, gentlemen,
and then I have a little announcement to make, yes . . .

(*There is another fanfare*)

STORYTELLER. Sir Oblong fitz Oblong!

(SIR OBLONG FITZ OBLONG *enters sadly. He is short, plump, with a
pink innocent face topped by a tonsure of white hair. He is pedantic and
almost priggy, and wears silver armour*)

DUKE. There you are, Oblong; mission accomplished?
OBLONG. Yes, Your Grace.
DUKE. Got the tail?
OBLONG. Yes, Your Grace.
DUKE (*kindly*) Well perk up, man. Whatever's the matter?
OBLONG (*producing a tail*) It was a very small dragon. Your Grace.
Small and, er, pink. I don't think it can have been fully grown. It
meant no harm I'm sure. (*He regards the small pink tail on table, then
takes a handkerchief from the sleeve of his armour and blows his nose*)
DUKE. Now Oblong, we all know how you feel about animals,
and I'm sure respect you for it. (*He looks round*)

(*There is a murmur of confirmation from the* KNIGHTS)

But—Duty First, eh?

OBLONG (*bracing*) Yes, Your Grace. (*He sits* L *of Duke*)

DUKE. That's it. (*Patting Oblong's shoulder as he sits*) Never knew an Oblong hold back in the face of duty. (*Briskly*) Now, Juniper my dear chap, read the next item on the agenda will you?

JUNIPER. Er, "Activities for the coming Season", Your Grace.

DUKE. Exactly! (*Rising*) Gentlemen, a happy announcement: There *are* no activities for the coming season. These (*the tails on the table*) were the last dragons in the Dukedom. Thanks to your untiring efforts over the years our peasantry may now reap their harvests—and pay their taxes—without interference. Our townsfolk can make their profits—and pay their taxes freely. And in short, there isn't a blessed thing for us to do.

(*The* KNIGHTS *rise and congratulate one another noisily shaking hands, patting backs, etc. The hubbub dies and they all sit*)

OBLONG. How perfectly splendid, Your Grace.

DUKE. Isn't it, isn't it?

OBLONG. Now we can move on somewhere else.

DUKE (*faintly*) Er, "move on", Oblong?

OBLONG. Yes, Your Grace.

DUKE. Whatever for?

OBLONG (*mildly puzzled*) To succour the poor and needy, Your Grace. Up North, for instance—dragons, barons, goblins. Having a very thin time of it up North, the poor and needy.

DUKE. But my dear fellow—the climate!

OBLONG. Well, South, then, Your Grace.

SMOOTHE (*gently*) May I say something, Your Grace?

DUKE. Smoothe! Yes! Please, please.

SMOOTHE. Well gentlemen, we've put this district into some sort of shape—and it's not been easy as you know. It seems to me we've earned a breather.

DUKE. Earned a breather. Well said, Smoothe. Late lie-in in the morning. Bit of jousting in the afternoon perhaps. Substantial supper; jolly good game of musical bumps and off to bed. (*Appealing all round*) Where's the harm in that?

(*A murmur of considered agreement*)

I'll put it to the vote. Democratic procedure—Can't say fairer than that, Oblong. All those in favour of the programme just outlined, please say "Aye".

ALL BUT OBLONG. Aye!

DUKE. Thank you. All those in favour of moving on, to wild, wet, baron and dragon infested areas, please say "Aye".

OBLONG. Er, Aye.

DUKE (*cheerfully*) Well there it is, old man. You're outvoted.

OBLONG (*diffident*) Under the terms of our Charter, Your Grace, I *think* a vote on this subject has to be unanimous. Nobody must disagree.

DUKE (*weakly*) That right?

JUNIPER (*looking at the Charter on the table*) I'm just looking . . . Yes, here it is, Your Grace, Clause Seven. (*He passes the Charter to the Duke*)

DUKE. Well . . . (*Petulantly*) Very ill-judged Clause, I would say. Now what?

JUNIPER. If we can't agree, Your Grace, we must refer the matter to the Royal Court.

STRONGBODY (*gloomily*) And we know what they'll say . . .

OBLONG. I'm sorry to be the fly in the ointment, gentlemen, but—to succour the poor and needy—dash it all gentlemen, it's our Knightly Vow!

(*At this, All look uncomfortably at the table. The small pink tail twitches slowly in the silence. ALL look. OBLONG is distressed*)

Oh dear; Your Grace, would you mind . . .

DUKE (*testy*) Yes, yes, take it away if it upsets you: take them *all* away.

(OBLONG *rises and picks up the tails*)

OBLONG (*muttering; embarrassed*) 'Scuse me, gentlemen—I—(*He moves to go, then turns. Apologetically*)—er—oh dear . . .

(OBLONG *exits with the tails, watched by all*)

JUNIPER. Well, there goes the late lie-in.

STRONGBODY. And the joustin'.

TRUMPINGTON. And the musical bumps.

JUNIPER. And the substantial suppers.

FIRST KNIGHT (*uneasy*) Got a point there, you know, about the Knightly Vow.

DUKE. Yes, yes; capital creature; heart of gold; but . . .

SMOOTHE. But inclined to be dogmatic, Your Grace.

DUKE. Exactly.

SMOOTHE. I think I see a possible solution.

(ALL *raise their heads and look to Smoothe*)

Supposing Oblong were to leave us. On a mission. A mission to—say—the Bolligrew Islands.

DUKE. The Bolligrew Islands!

FIRST KNIGHT. I say, that's a bit steep.

TRUMPINGTON. D'you think he'd go?

JUNIPER. It's worth trying. Your Grace might have him appointed a Royal Knight Errant.

DUKE. And then when he'd gone we could put the matter to the vote again and—er . . . ?

JUNIPER. And nobody would disagree!

DUKE. Unanimous vote, as required by our Charter!

SMOOTHE. Exactly, Your Grace.

DUKE (*solemnly*) There's no doubt, gentlemen, the Bolligrew Islands *need* a Knight Errant.

JUNIPER. Unquestionably.

DUKE. And Oblong is the obvious choice.

FIRST KNIGHT. That's true.

DUKE. I dare say he'll be very happy there.

(SMOOTHE *coughs warningly.* OBLONG *enters*)

Oblong my dear chap, what would you say to the idea of a mission to the Bolligrew Islands?

OBLONG. I should say it was a very *good* idea, Your Grace! When do we start?

DUKE. Well, we were thinking of a—more of a—one man mission, you know.

OBLONG. Oh. Me?

DUKE. Yes. Smoothe here suggested you.

OBLONG (*sharply*) Very good of you, Smoothe. I'm not going.

DUKE. "Not", Oblong?

OBLONG. No! The Bolligrew Islands! That's where Baron-Bolligrew lives—the one that pulled down the church!

DUKE (*shocked*) Did he really? I didn't know that.

OBLONG. Well he did. And there's that dragon in the Bolligrew Islands too.

SMOOTHE. A very *poor* specimen, I believe.

OBLONG. It isn't. It's one of those black ones with red eyes.

FIRST KNIGHT (*uncomfortably*) It's a bit steep, you know.

SMOOTHE. Quite right, quite right. We ought not to persuade Sir Oblong.

(OBLONG *moves to his chair but is stopped by Smoothe's next words*)

It is a pity, though. I understand that Baron Bolligrew hunts.

OBLONG (*sharply*) Hunts?

SMOOTHE (*looking up in mock surprise*) Er, hunts, yes.

OBLONG (*suspiciously*) What does he hunt?

SMOOTHE (*looking to the Duke*) Pretty well anything, they say.

DUKE. Foxes.

SMOOTHE (*nodding*) Foxes, bears—

TRUMPINGTON. Deer—

JUNIPER. Badgers—

OBLONG. Oh the villain!

SMOOTHE (*offhand*) Hares, of course—little, trembling hares. . .

OBLONG. It—really it makes one's blood boil!

SMOOTHE. Your Grace, if Sir Oblong *were* going on this mission I expect His Majesty would make him a Royal Knight Errant, don't you?

DUKE. Couldn't refuse. And then you could wear the purple robe, you know, with the Royal Coat of Arms and so on. I think Oblong would look well in purple, don't you, Juniper?

OBLONG (*taken with it*) Really? I must say—hares and badgers you say?

SMOOTHE. Oh anything.

OBLONG. The perfect brute! Your Grace, I'll go.

DUKE. Excellent conclusion to a good morning's work, gentlemen. How about a little refreshment?

STORYTELLER. Lemonade and ice-cream on the South Terrace!

DUKE. Meeting adjourned!

(*The* DUKE *and* KNIGHTS *exit, rolling the table with them. The* LIGHTS *go out, except for the single spot* C *as the* STORYTELLER *moves below it*)

STORYTELLER. So Sir Oblong was appointed a Royal Knight Errant and at length—

(*A brown paper parcel is thrown on from wings and caught by the* STORYTELLER)

—a parcel from the King's Court arrived at the Duke's Castle— (*he opens the parcel*)—containing Sir Oblong's purple robe.

(OBLONG *enters into the spot, and is assisted into the robe by the* STORYTELLER.)

Sir Oblong put it on and he found a berth on a ship—

(*The* CAPTAIN *enters carrying a* "*mast and sail*")

—which was making the short but dangerous passage to the Bolligrew Islands.

(*The* CAPTAIN *and* OBLONG *traverse the stage, there is a lightning flash and a thunderclap, in cover of which the* STORYTELLER *exits*)

The LIGHTS *come up*

OBLONG. These are the Bolligrew Islands are they, Captain?

CAPTAIN. Yus. 'Orrible aren't they? See the ruin up there? That's the church Baron Bolligrew pulled down some years back.

OBLONG. He's a difficult man to get on with, I believe.

CAPTAIN. 'Orrible. That's not the worst of it neither.

OBLONG. No?

CAPTAIN. No. See that 'illside; all black and smoky like?

OBLONG. Oh yes.

CAPTAIN. Dragon.

OBLONG. I beg your pardon?

CAPTAIN. Dragon done it. Breathin' fire like. 'Orrible.

OBLONG. Doesn't Baron Bolligrew do anything about it?

CAPTAIN. Not 'im. 'Untin's all 'e cares about. 'Untin' and grindin' the faces of the poor. Reg'lar terror. You thinkin' of settlin' 'ere?

OBLONG. Er, well I was, yes . . .

CAPTAIN. Wouldn't live 'ere for a million pounds myself. 'Ere we are 'owever. If you'll just stand on one side, sir. Ava-a-a-ast! Bel-a-a-ay! (*He pulls a cord, the sail furls*) There you are sir, now you can go ashore and . . . (*There is a crash of a shotgun off stage*) Look out! 'Ere 'e is.

(JASPER, 15TH BARON BOLLIGREW *enters, carrying a twelve-bore shotgun. He is small but burly, with a red face and black whiskers; choleric and selfish but with the fascination of childish greed. He is anachronistically dressed in a loud check jacket, bowler hat, breeches, gaiters. He walks deliberately to the others. Accompanying him is* SQUIRE BLACKHEART, *huge and stupid. He wears black armour topped by enormous black plumes. He moons stolidly throughout the interview, chewing his moustache*)

BOLLIGREW. Missed 'im. You Captain Asquith of the ship *Winkle*?

CAPTAIN. Yes, my lord.

BOLLIGREW. You brought me a new whip?

CAPTAIN. Yes, me lord.

BOLLIGREW. New spurs?

CAPTAIN. Yes, me lord.

BOLLIGREW. New boots?

CAPTAIN. Boots, me lord?

BOLLIGREW. Yes, boots. Me new ridin' boots.

CAPTAIN. They didn't say nothin' about no boots, me lord.

BOLLIGREW. Ho, didn't they?

CAPTAIN. No, me lord.

BOLLIGREW. Well you go back and get 'em.

CAPTAIN (*glancing fearfully back at the "voyage" just made*) But me lord . . .

BOLLIGREW. Don't argue with *me*, Asquith. Just turn your ship round and get me boots.

CAPTAIN. Yes, me lord.

(*The* CAPTAIN *hoists sail and exits to more thunder and lightning, watched by* ALL)

BOLLIGREW. Insolent beggar! Who might you be?

OBLONG. Oblong fitz Oblong.

BOLLIGREW. Gentleman?

OBLONG. Yes?

BOLLIGREW. Me friend, Squire Blackheart.

BLACKHEART. 'D'you do?

OBLONG. How . . .

BOLLIGREW. Knight Errant, eh?

OBLONG. Yes. (*Modestly*) A recent appointment.

BOLLIGREW. Knight Errant, Blackheart.

(BLACKHEART *grunts and nods gloomily*)

BOLLIGREW. D'you hunt?

OBLONG. Well, as a matter of . . .

BOLLIGREW. I do.

OBLONG. Yes, I hear you're a keen sportsman, Baron.

BOLLIGREW. Keen sportsman. Right. (*Lugging out an enormous gold watch*). See that? "Presented to the Master of Bolligrew Hounds" —that's me, of course "as a mark of admiration and gratitude, by the Chairman of the Hunt Committee". Handsome timepiece, eh?

OBLONG. Lovely. Who is the Chairman of the Hunt Committee?

BOLLIGREW. I am. Solid gold that watch. Had to evict three or four entire families to pay for it, didn't we, Blackheart?

BLACKHEART. Mm.

BOLLIGREW. Blackheart does all the evictin' work round here. (*Replacing the watch*) Well. Give you a day tomorrow if you like. We're after a badger.

OBLONG. Baron Bolligrew, I do not hunt!

(*There is a short silence*)

BOLLIGREW. Doesn't hunt, Blackheart.

(BLACKHEART *grunts and nods gloomily*)

BOLLIGREW (*to Oblong*) Afraid of horses, very likely.

OBLONG (*stiffly*) Some of my best friends are horses . . .

BOLLIGREW. Feller's potty, Blackheart.

BLACKHEART. Hey!

BOLLIGREW. What?

BLACKHEART. Magpie.

(BOLLIGREW *raises his gun.* ALL *follow a flight of an unseen bird above, then* OBLONG *"accidentally" steps backwards onto Bolligrew's foot.* BOLLIGREW *roars and the gun roars.* BOLLIGREW *hops, furious, watched apprehensively by* OBLONG. BLACKHEART, *oblivious, continues to watch the flight of the bird, off*)

BOLLIGREW (*eyeing Oblong narrowly*) Did you do that on purpose? He did that on purpose, Blackheart.

BLACKHEART (*lowering his gaze to Bolligrew*) What?

BOLLIGREW. He trod on my toe. (*Still eyeing Oblong narrowly*) Now, look here, Oblong, if you don't 'unt, what've you come for?

OBLONG (*searching his armour for the paper*) I have my instructions somewhere. (*Putting on his spectacles*) It's all pretty run-of-the-mill stuff. (*Clearing his throat*) Item: rebuild Bolligrew Island Church. Item: Restore justice to Bolligrew Island Magistrates Court. Item: Suppress Bolligrew Island Dragon.

(BOLLIGREW *listens with mounting indignation but now laughs*)

BOLLIGREW. Suppress . . .? Feller's goin' to suppress the dragon, Blackheart!

(BLACKHEART *grins, the grin broadens, he breaks into guffaws*)

BOLLIGREW. And—and—restore justice to—to the Magistrates Court!

(BOLLIGREW *and* BLACKHEART *hold on to each other, helpless*)

(*to Oblong, wiping his eyes*) Here, here—you like to see the Court in session?

OBLONG. At the earliest opportunity, Baron.

BOLLIGREW. Nothing easier. (*He takes a whistle from his pocket and blows*)

(*The* RAGGED PEASANTRY *enter. They are barefoot, and dressed in ragged clothes of sacking. Two* MEN-AT-ARMS *follow, with a bench which they put down. They wear conventional medieval costume, surcoats bearing the golden toad of the Bolligrews. Last comes the* LORD MAYOR. *He is a timid man, wearing slightly less ragged peasant costume, with shoes, and topped by a waistcoat and his Chain of Office*)

Ready, Blackheart old man?

BLACKHEART. Ready when you are, my dear feller.

(BLACKHEART *and* BOLLIGREW *sit*)

There you are, Oblong. Court's in session.

(OBLONG *sits*)

BOLLIGREW. What the blazes do you think you're doing?

OBLONG. I am taking my seat on the Bench, Baron.

BOLLIGREW. And who the blazes gave you a seat on the Bench?

OBLONG. My Royal Commission gives me a seat on the Bench, Baron.

BOLLIGREW. Oh. (*Recovering*) Well that's all right. We don't mind, do we, Blackheart?

BLACKHEART. Don't we?

BOLLIGREW. No. Loyal subjects of His Majesty, Blackheart and me, Oblong—hope you'll notice that. Right—First Case!

(*The* MEN-AT-ARMS *seize a diminutive* PEASANT)

FIRST MAN-AT-ARMS. First case!

PEASANT (*fearfully*) Here, my lord.

SECOND MAN-AT-ARMS. First case present, my lord!

BOLLIGREW. What's the charge?

FIRST MAN-AT-ARMS. On the last day of last month, my lord, at about tea-time, prisoner was seen to prevent a horse from eating a double row of runner beans in 'is garden.

BOLLIGREW. Oh. But look here, why *should* he let horses eat his runner beans?

FIRST MAN-AT-ARMS (*slightly shocked*) 'Twas your horse, my lord.

BOLLIGREW. Was it! Guilty!

OBLONG. *Not* guilty!

BOLLIGREW. Squire Blackheart, what do you think?

BLACKHEART. Guilty. Definitely.

BOLLIGREW. That's two to one. Seven days bread and water and —let's see, prisoner aren't you the one with the strawberry bed?

PEASANT. I 'ave got a few strawberry plants, my lord, yes . . .

BOLLIGREW. Good—and a fine of three baskets of strawberries. You can deliver them to the Castle—back door, mind—after you've served your sentence. Next case.

MAN-AT-ARMS. Here, my lord.

BOLLIGREW. You?

MAN-AT-ARMS. Yes, my lord.

BOLLIGREW. But that's one of your men, isn't it Blackheart?

BLACKHEART (*affixing a monocle*) It is. It's my Second Huntsman.

BOLLIGREW. Who's had the blazin' impudence to charge this man?

LORD MAYOR (*timidly determined*) Er, me, my lord.

BOLLIGREW. You Lord Mayor? Well, I can only say that I'm surprised.

LORD MAYOR. My lord, if you feel that my bringing the case is in any way disrespectful, of course . . .

BOLLIGREW (*holding up a solemn hand*) This is a Court of Law. Case is brought now, Lord Mayor, and must just go forward for an impartial hearing. So let's hear whatever cock-and-bull story you've cooked up.

LORD MAYOR. Well, yesterday morning, my lord, I was in my sweet-shop when I saw this fellow coming along the High Street with a number of dogs.

BLACKHEART. Hounds, Lord Mayor. We call 'em hounds.

LORD MAYOR. Hounds. Thank you. (*He clears his throat, then continues to Bolligrew*) He came into my shop, took down a jar of best quality humbugs and gave them to these hounds . . .!

BLACKHEART (*his brow clearing*) Oh that's all right, Lord Mayor! Wouldn't do 'em any harm. Hounds like humbugs. Often noticed it myself.

LORD MAYOR (*querulous*) Very well, Squire; if you can afford to give your hounds best quality humbugs at fourpence a quarter, very well. But my point is this—do you think your man paid for them? He did not. (*Shrill*) He never does!

BOLLIGREW (*weakly*) Blackheart, I don't think I can be followin'. Is he suggestin' that your man should *pay* for his humbugs?

BLACKHEART. That your point, Lord Mayor?

LORD MAYOR. It is, Squire, yes.

BLACKHEART. Seems to be a deuced ugly spirit about, old man.

BOLLIGREW. Well I—I'm dumbfounded, Blackheart. I leave it to you.

BLACKHEART. Case dismissed.

BOLLIGREW. Yes? Very well, then. Lord Mayor, I personally take the gravest possible view of this incident. But in the light of my colleague's recommendation to mercy and your hitherto excellent record, I will dismiss you with a caution. Next case!

OBLONG. But this is scandalous!

BOLLIGREW (*nodding; humbly*) You're probably right, Oblong. I tell you frankly, I'm too soft-hearted to be a good Magistrate. (*jovially*) Ah—it's you, Bobblenob. Brought me money?

OBIDIAH. No, my lord. (*He kneels*) Mercy . . .

OBLONG. Will somebody please tell me the circumstances of this case?

BOLLIGREW. Ah yes. The circumstances my dear chap are as follows. About ten months ago this man, Obidiah Bobblenob, wilfully and maliciously chucked half a brick through one of my greenhouses . . .

OBIDIAH. No my lord! Beg pardon my lord, but I didn't, really I didn't!

BOLLIGREW. You see the sort of chap he is, Oblong; thoroughly hardened character; refuses to admit it even now. Without the slightest provocation he pitches a brick through my greenhouse. And what did I do? I fined 'im a pound. One miserable pound. I think you'll agree I was lenient.

OBLONG. How do you make your living, Obidiah?

OBIDIAH. I'm an egg-painter by trade, sir. I sells 'ard-boiled eggs in the market, with designs and funny faces painted on them in different colours.

BOLLIGREW. And a very profitable line it is, as I expect you know!

OBLONG. Then did you pay your fine?

OBIDIAH. No sir, I couldn't!

OBLONG. Why not?

BOLLIGREW. It's a funny thing is that. It seems he had his eggs all ready for market, and the night before some hooligan broke into his cottage and smashed 'em up. That's right, isn't it, Bobblenob?

OBIDIAH (*whispers*) Yes, my lord.

BOLLIGREW. Mm. So you see, Oblong, when the next Court came round he couldn't pay. However, I wasn't disposed to be hard on him—the Bobblenobs have lived on the estate for generations. Pretty little house Bobblenob lives in—got a pond in the garden, hasn't it, Bobblenob?

OBIDIAH. Yes, my lord.

BOLLIGREW. Yes. (*Briskly*) So all I did was to add another pound to the fine, and leave it at that. (*He smiles complacently at Oblong, as one expecting approval.*)

OBLONG. So then he owed you *two* pounds.

BOLLIGREW (*calculating*) Er, one and one—two. Yes exactly two pounds.

OBLONG. And then what?

BOLLIGREW. Well, Oblong, it's an extraordinary thing but the same thing happened again.

OBLONG. So he couldn't pay the fine again.

BOLLIGREW. Exactly—

OBLONG. So you added another pound—

BOLLIGREW. Making three.

OBLONG. And then it happened again.

BOLLIGREW. You're right, my dear chap; it did!

OBLONG. And it's gone on happening ever since.

BOLLIGREW. My dear Oblong, what a brain you must have!

OBLONG. And who is the mysterious "hooligan" who breaks in and smashes Obidiah's eggs every day before market day, so that he can't pay his fine on Court day?

BOLLIGREW. I've no idea. Have you Bobblenob?

OBIDIAH (*after a fractional hesitation*) No my Lord.

BOLLIGREW. Well now: It's nine so far so to-day makes it ten. Nice round number. Ten pounds next Court, Bobblenob. Let's see, there's a market to-morrow morning, isn't there? We'll have a special Court for you that afternoon. And see what you can do at the market, there's a good chap.

OBIDIAH (*whispers*) Yes, my lord.

BOLLIGREW. That's it. I'm relying on you, Bobblenob to save me from a painful duty. (*He digs Blackheart in the ribs and laughs*)

(BLACKHEART *stares at him woodenly.* BOLLIGREW *stops laughing, turns to Oblong, sighs*)

I'm wasted on Black'eart, I really am. Well—Last Case?

MAN-AT-ARMS. *Last* case, my Lord!

BOLLIGREW. Court will rise!

(BOLLIGREW *and* BLACKHEART *rise, then* OBLONG)

And you can all clear off.

(ALL *except* BLACKHEART, BOLLIGREW *and* OBLONG *exit hurriedly, the* MEN-AT-ARMS *taking the bench.* BOLLIGREW *takes a cigar from his pocket and lights it*)

(*Insolently*) Got the picture?

OBLONG. I have indeed.

BOLLIGREW (*nodding sympathetically*) There's nothing *you* can do here, Oblong. Go back where you came from, eh?

OBLONG. Baron, Squire—I wish you good-day. (*He turns to go*)

BOLLIGREW. Oblong!

(OBLONG *turns.* BOLLIGREW *approaches, pointing at him, warningly*)

I've a short way with Knights Errant.

OBLONG. Well, I've a fairly short way with Barons. Good-day.

(OBLONG *exits.* BOLLIGREW *looks after him thoughtfully. He turns and looks at Blackheart.* BLACKHEART *is mindlessly gazing over the audience, sucking one end of his moustache.* BOLLIGREW *approaches him*)

BOLLIGREW. Blackheart. (*Handing him a cigar*) Have a cigar.

BLACKHEART. Mm? Oh, thanks. (*He takes the cigar*)

BOLLIGREW (*lighting his cigar*) We shall have trouble with that feller, Blackheart.

BLACKHEART. Little fat feller just now?

BOLLIGREW. That's the one. He, er—

(*He takes* BLACKHEART *by the elbow; they patrol downstage, smoking cigars*)

He fancies himself as a bit of a fighter for one thing.

BLACKHEART (*interested*) Oh?

BOLLIGREW. Mm. Didn't you notice how he kept lookin' at you?

BLACKHEART. No?

BOLLIGREW. Oh.

BLACKHEART (*anxiously*) How was he lookin' at me?

BOLLIGREW. Well you know, like he thought you were a big bag of wind.

BLACKHEART. What?

BOLLIGREW. Mm, you know—like he thought you were a big feller but not much good in a scrap.

BLACKHEART. He didn't!

BOLLIGREW. He did. I wondered how you could put up with it. "How does Blackheart put up with it," that's what I kept wonderin'. I mean it's not the thing, is it, for a gentleman to put up with that?

BLACKHEART (*going*) I'll flatten 'im!

BOLLIGREW. Er—Blackheart.

(BLACKHEART *turns.* BOLLIGREW *beckons him back*)

There *is* a complication.

BLACKHEART. Oh?

BOLLIGREW. Mm. This feller's a Royal Knight Errant, ye see. Got the purple mantle.

BLACKHEART. *I*'m not afraid of . . .

BOLLIGREW. No, no, no—of course you're not. But—we could have trouble from the mainland you see. I mean, we don't want a Royal Commission, do we? I mean, we don't want the Islands *swarming* with Knights Errant, poking their long noses into every blazin' thing, do we?

BLACKHEART (*sobered*) Goo' Lor' no. Better leave 'im alone, eh?

BOLLIGREW. Mmm—don't know about that. You *are* a gentleman.

BLACKHEART (*laughing*) Well, I should 'ope so!

BOLLIGREW. Yes. Well then, you're entitled to satisfaction. But, just make sure you do it in the proper form.

BLACKHEART. Right. (*He glances off uneasily, then draws close to Bolligrew*) What *is* the proper form?

BOLLIGREW. Oh. Well. First, you must throw down the gauntlet.

BLACKHEART (*gazing at it*) Me gauntlet.

BOLLIGREW. That's it. Chuck it down. That's a challenge. Then if he picks it up . . .

BLACKHEART. Yes?

BOLLIGREW. You can clobber him.

BLACKHEART. Right.

BOLLIGREW. If he *don't* pick it up . . .

BLACKHEART. Yes?

BOLLIGREW. Then insult him. And if he *still* won't fight . . .

BLACKHEART. Yes?

BOLLIGREW. Then you can't touch him.

BLACKHEART. Well what's the good of that?

BOLLIGREW. Ah. You see, old man, you must do it in front of witnesses. This feller, ye see, has set himself up as the Champion of the poor and needy. And if 'e won't fight after *that* . . .

BLACKHEART. Yes?

BOLLIGREW. Well then, his sweaty friends will see what sort of Champion they've got! Won't they?

BLACKHEART (*with a grunt*) Yes, but look 'ere, where's me satisfaction?

BOLLIGREW. That, Blackheart, would satisfy any gentleman that ever breathed.

BLACKHEART. Oh. Right. Let's have it again. That's gauntlet, insult, sweaty . . . ?

BOLLIGREW (*looking at him dubiously*) Tell you what. Come up to the castle and I'll jot it down for you.

BLACKHEART. Oh. Right.

(BLACKHEART *and* BOLLIGREW *move to exit, as the* STORYTELLER *enters, meeting them. He is struggling on with the Church ruins*)

BOLLIGREW. Evening.

STORYTELLER. Good evening, Baron.

BOLLIGREW. What you got there then?

STORYTELLER. The ruins of Bolligrew Church, Baron. We shall need them for the next scene.

BOLLIGREW. Church ruins, Blackheart. Thought they looked familiar.

STORYTELLER (*pausing; breathless*) I wonder if the Squire would. . . ?

BLACKHEART. My good man, I'm not a bally labourer.

BOLLIGREW. Quite right. You' got any heavin' and liftin' to do, find a bally peasant!

(BLACKHEART *and* BOLLIGREW *exit*)

STORYTELLER (*calling off*) Sir Oblong!

(OBLONG *enters*)

STORYTELLER. I wonder if you'd . . .

OBLONG. Of course.

(*They lug the ruins into place*)

Church ruins, eh?

STORYTELLER. Yes, we need them for the next scene.

OBLONG. Mm, pretty. Must have been a pretty little place—I shall enjoy the first part of my mission. (*Anxiously*) However, I shall need assistance . . .

STORYTELLER. The poor and needy?

OBLONG. Excellent.

(*The STORYTELLER addresses the audience*)

STORYTELLER. The poor and needy of the Island, when they heard that he had come to be their champion, flocked in upon the gallant Knight from every side!

(*The PEASANTS and LORD MAYOR enter, OBLONG addresses them. The STORYTELLER exits*)

OBLONG. Poor and needy, Lord Mayor. I have been sent here by the Duke to help you. Will you help me?

(*Dubious agreement from the PEASANTS*)

PEASANTS
{ Don't see why not . . .
{ Give it a go . . .
{ 'pends what kind of 'elp 'e wants,

OBLONG. In the first place I want information. Tell me something about Squire Blackheart. (*He notes down their replies*)

FIRST PEASANT. 'E's a 'ard case is the Squire, sir.

SECOND PEASANT. You know that black armour of his, sir?

OBLONG. Yes?

SECOND PEASANT. Never takes it off, sir.

THIRD PEASANT. 'E sleeps in it.

OBLONG (*noting it all down and nodding gravely*) One of those, is he? Now what about the Dragon?

(*On the word "Dragon" the PEASANTS scatter: stop: return*)

FIRST PEASANT. 'Ere. Don't you go near Dragon, now.

SECOND PEASANT. Gobble you up like a raspberry, 'e will.

THIRD PEASANT. Baron 'isself is afeared of Dragon.

OBLONG. My understanding was that the Baron has some sort of arrangement with the Dragon.

FOURTH PEASANT. So 'e 'as, sir. Baron as this side of the Island for grindin' the faces of the poor, and Dragon 'as that side of the Island for ravagin'. That's the agreement. But I reckon the Baron be afeared of 'e all the same . . .

OBLONG. Matters here are worse than I had realized. (*He flips shut his notebook*) Now my first task is to rebuild this church. May I count on your assistance?

FIRST PEASANT. Baron isn't goin' to like that, sir.

SECOND PEASANT. 'E doan' 'old wi' churches, sir.

THIRD PEASANT. I mean, 'e pulled it down; stands to reason 'e doan' want it buildin' up again.

OBLONG. If we are to consult the likes and dislikes of the Baron at every turn, we shall accomplish very little.

(*There is an awkward silence*)

Remember—you will be under the protection of the Duke.

FIFTH PEASANT. Meanin' no disrespect sir, but Duke's a long way away. We ain't never seen Duke in the Islands, sir.

OBLONG. That is a just observation . . . (*He considers, mounts the ruin, and addresses them, Crispin's Day fashion*) There was a time when the peasants of this island were a byword for their fearlessness and sturdy independence! In time of Peace they followed the plough with straight backs and heads high!

(*The* PEASANTS *unconsciously straighten their backs*)

In time of War—

(*The* PEASANTS *unconsciously fall into martial postures*)

—they pressed as though by instinct even to the thickest of the fray, hard after the great banner of the Bolligrew the Golden Toad, and were a terror to the very cream of foreign chivalry!

PEASANTS (*carried away*) Hurrah!

OBLONG. These were your fathers! Are you their sons?

PEASANTS. Yes!

OBLONG. Then do we build the church?

PEASANTS. We do!

OBLONG. Then (*pointing dramatically*) building materials!

PEASANTS. Building materials!

(*The* PEASANTS *rush off enthusiastically*)

LORD MAYOR. A wonderful gift for words you have.

OBLONG. Oh it's all part of our training you know, where do *you* stand on this business.

LORD MAYOR. You understand, Sir Oblong, I'm—er—delicately situated.

OBLONG. I do see that.

LORD MAYOR. If there's anything I can do in proper form . . .

OBLONG. I understand.

LORD MAYOR. But I can hardly take part in, well, a popular uprising.

OBLONG. You're delicately situated.

LORD MAYOR. Thank you. Er—(*He edges closer to Oblong*)— between ourselves, you've put your finger on the nub of the matter with this fellow Blackheart. Between ourselves—(*glancing about*)— not really out of the top drawer.

OBLONG. No?

LORD MAYOR. No. For all his moustaches. His father—(*he glances around again*)—his father was an underfootman in the late Lord Bolligrew's time.

OBLONG. Really?

LORD MAYOR. I remember him. I went to school with Squire Blackheart so-called. An inveterate bully, Sir Oblong, and backward in his lessons, very backward . . .

(*The* LORD MAYOR *breaks off as the noise of the* PEASANTS *approaches. The* PEASANTS *enter bearing sections of the Church: one with a wheelbarrow, one with a stepladder*)

FIRST PEASANT (*breathlessly*) There you are, sir!

SECOND PEASANT. Building materials!

OBLONG. Splendid! (*He inspects the contents of the wheelbarrow*) Mortar and trowel. Splendid, splendid. (*He takes the handles of the barrow*) Now then. For your manhood and your ancient liberties. Forward!

(OBLONG *steps out rhetorically with the barrow, followed by the* PEASANTS, *but stops instantly as* BLACKHEART *enters. The* STORY-TELLER *enters separately at the same moment, and watches soberly*)

Good evening, Squire.

BLACKHEART. Tchah!

(BLACKHEART *advances deliberately, the* PEASANTS *shrinking back, and hurls down his gauntlet*)

OBLONG. You've dropped your glove.

BLACKHEART. I've thrown down me gauntlet. Any gentleman'd know that.

OBLONG. You want me to fight a duel with you, Squire?

BLACKHEART. Right.

OBLONG. Well, I'm not going to.

BLACKHEART. Then—(*an effort of memory*)—I'm goin' to insult you!

OBLONG. Well please be quick; I have a lot to do and the light's going.

BLACKHEART (*studying a grubby scrap of paper*) Oblong, you're a—a, mm . . . (*He has difficulty in reading*)

(OBLONG *peers at the paper*)

OBLONG. Varlet.

BLACKHEART. Right! A varlet! And a, mm . . .

OBLONG. Knave.

BLACKHEART. That's it! Knave and varlet! You—you're not a gentleman! Thought of that meself.

OBLONG. The subject seems to obsess you, Squire.

BLACKHEART (*amazed*) Well, if you won't fight *now* . . .

OBLONG. No.

(BLACKHEART, *nonplussed, consults the paper, then his brow clears*)

BLACKHEART. Well then, your sweaty friends can see what kind of Champion they've *got*! (*To the Fifth Peasant*) You.
FIFTH PEASANT (*approaching; humbly*) Yes, Squire?
BLACKHEART. Pick up me glove.
FIFTH PEASANT. Yes, Squire. (*He does so*)

(*Behind Oblong, the* PEASANTS *lay down the sections of the church*)

BLACKHEART (*to Oblong; going*) And a very good evening to *you* Fatty!

(BLACKHEART *exits. The* PEASANTS *start to leave in the opposite direction*)

OBLONG (*watching Blackheart off*) What a deplorable exhibition! Well now—(*turning to find the Peasants going*) What's the matter? Stop!

(*All the* PEASANTS *exit except the* FIFTH)

My good friend . . .
FIFTH PEASANT (*following the others*) Sorry, sir. But if you'm afeared to tackle Squire, we'm afeared to 'elp you. And that's the top and bottom of it, sir.

(*The* FIFTH PEASANT *exits*)

OBLONG (*to the Lord Mayor*) I'm not afraid of the Squire!
LORD MAYOR. No, no. Of course not.
OBLONG. But duelling is utterly against my principles.
LORD MAYOR. I agree with you, Sir Oblong, I agree with you. (*But he is backing towards the exit*)
OBLONG. Well, the two of us must just do what we can, eh? (*Attempting to lift a large segment of the church*) Would you . . . ?
LORD MAYOR. The fact is, sir, I ought to be getting back to the shop, I'm sorry, Sir Oblong, really I am . . .

(*The* LORD MAYOR *exits*)

OBLONG. Dash it! (*Defiantly*) Yes—I am not often intemperate in my language but *dash* it! What shall I do now?
STORYTELLER. I'm afraid I can't tell you.
OBLONG. But you're the Storyteller aren't you?
STORYTELLER. I am the Storyteller, yes.
OBLONG. Well what happens next in the story?
STORYTELLER. What happens next, Sir Oblong, is that you are left on your own.

(*The* STORYTELLER *exits*)

OBLONG. Well that's very inconvenient! (*He appeals to the audience*) What shall I do? Perhaps I ought to have fought that fellow Blackheart after all? What do you think? (*He continues ad lib till the audience response is strong*) Might do him good to learn a lesson, eh? In my younger days I was national Broadsword Champion you know, and—and Area Champion three years running! (*Growing excited*) After all, he challenged me, didn't he? Perhaps I ought to find the fellow now? Do a little challenging myself? Ha! (*Drawing his sword*) Have at thee for a foul catiff! Take that—and that—anthatanthatanthat! (*When the response is at its maximum, he pulls himself up*) No. No. (*He sheathes his sword*) Certainly not. I have been sent here to set a good example. You ought to be ashamed of yourselves. Duelling, is *wrong* . . . I must manage somehow by myself. (*Attempting to lift a segment of the church*). No. Now let's see—no. You know at this point in the story I do think they might send *somebody* to help me.

(MAGPIE *enters, unseen by Oblong. He is excitable and amoral, and wears a lifelike costume of pied feathers*)

However! Keep trying—no.
A VOICE FROM THE AUDIENCE. Behind you!
OBLONG. What? Try a smaller piece? Right. Now, then . . . No. I really don't see how I'm going to manage, you know. How about this bit . . . ? (*And so on, till the audience response is strong. Then he turns, and sees Magpie*)
OBLONG. Oh. Good Evening.
MAGPIE. You talk.
OBLONG. Certainly.
MAGPIE. Most human beings only twitter.
OBLONG. Most human beings would say most birds only twitter.
MAGPIE. Eh?
OBLONG. Man. As a matter of fact, all human beings talk, among themselves.

(*The* LIGHTS *start to dim*)

MAGPIE. Don't believe it.
OBLONG. Well that's rather narrow minded of you. It takes all sorts to make a world you know.
MAGPIE. My name's Mike Magpie. Your name's Oblong. You saved my life this morning.
OBLONG. Oh, was that you?
MAGPIE. Awk.
OBLONG. He might have missed, you know.
MAGPIE. Not 'im. You saved my life an' you can count on me.
OBLONG. For what?
MAGPIE. Anything! I'm a pretty smart character.
OBLONG. Are you now?
MAGPIE. Oh yes. Brilliant bird—always have been.
OBLONG. Well the immediate task is to rebuild this church.
MAGPIE. Oh! Like, lugging stones about?

OBLONG. Yes?

MAGPIE. Like—work?

OBLONG. Yes, Michael, work.

MAGPIE. Well look 'ere, Obby, work's not in my line. Anythin' in the thieving line now, or the telling lies line, or the leading up the garden path line . . .

OBLONG. Did you say "thieving"?

MAGPIE. Yes. You know—pinching things.

OBLONG (*quietly*) What things?

MAGPIE. Shiny things. They're in my nest. 'D'you like to see?

OBLONG (*mounting the ladder to the nest on top of the tower*) Yes Michael, I should.

MAGPIE. Hey! You're not going to take my shiny things, are you?

OBLONG. Yours, Michael? (*Peering into the nest*) Mm. I am on the whole relieved. Silver paper, bits of glass—but there is a silver tie-pin with a fox head on it which appears to be of some value.

MAGPIE. That's all right; that's Bolligrew's!

OBLONG (*descending*) It makes not an atom of difference whose it is. Stealing is *wrong*.

MAGPIE. It's no good talking to me about right and wrong, Obby. It's not in my nature.

OBLONG. I know it's difficult for Magpies, Michael, but I want you to try. Imagine the impression it would make in the Islands if it were thought that I associated with a bird—I am sorry to say this—a bird of loose principles.

MAGPIE. Awk.

OBLONG. No more stealing then.

MAGPIE. Aw . . .

(*There is a noise off*)

Awk! A person!

OBLONG. Hide.

(MAGPIE *climbs to his nest.* OBLONG *peers off, hand on sword. A light approaches*)

Who's that?

(OBIDIAH *enters with a lamp*)

OBIDIAH. It's me, sir. Bobblenob the egg painter.

OBLONG. Ah, Obidiah. My poor friend, I'm sorry I wasn't able to help you in Court this morning.

OBIDIAH. You did your best sir, and I thanks you for it. That's what I come to say, sir.

OBLONG. There's no chance of your having the ten pounds by next Court Day, I suppose?

OBIDIAH. How can a poor man like me come by ten pounds, sir?

OBLONG. If I had any money myself I'd give it to you, Obidiah, willingly. But I haven't. We're not allowed to, you know.

OBIDIAH. I know that, sir. I've sometimes thought if Knights Errant were provided with proper funds, sir, they might make more of an impression, sir.

OBLONG. It's not for us to question the regulation, Obidiah.

OBIDIAH. No sir.

OBLONG. Can't you possibly make some eggs to sell at tomorrow's market?

OBIDIAH. I'd need a power of eggs to make ten pounds. And then again it's fiddlin' work, sir, is egg painting, and I couldn't get 'em finished by tomorrow, sir, if I 'ad 'em.

OBLONG. No. I suppose not.

OBIDIAH. And what if I did, sir, they'd only be smashed up again like the others.

OBLONG. Have you no idea who it is that breaks into your cottage and smashes up your eggs?

OBIDIAH. I *know* who it is, sir. It's Squire Blackheart.

OBLONG. Squire Blackheart! Obidiah, do you know what you are saying?

OBIDIAH. I seen 'im at it, sir, plain as I see you. But what can I do with a great strong gentleman like that? Well, sir, you yourself—I mean, you 'esitate don't you?

OBLONG. I hesitate no longer, Obidiah. (*He paces about restlessly*) I find myself agitated. (*He stops*) It's Baron Bolligrew who sends him, of course?

OBIDIAH. That's right, sir. T'isn't the money he wants, sir. 'Tis my cottage he's after. When he's raised the fine to fifteen pounds or thereabouts 'e'll take the cottage instead.

OBLONG. I see. Or rather, no I don't see. What on earth does Baron Bolligrew want with a cottage?

OBIDIAH. Well, sir; this pond goes with the cottage—and there's trout in this pond, sir.

OBLONG. Aha!

OBIDIAH. Yes, sir. Baron an' Squire been keen fishermen many a year now. Mine be last trout in the Islands near enough. And finer, happier fish you never did see. I feeds 'em night and morning, sir, same as my father did before me. Friends of the family, they are, in a manner of speakin', sir.

OBLONG (*looking at him sharply*) You converse with them, Obidiah?

OBIDIAH. Nothing I likes better of an evening, sir, than a quiet chat with they trout.

OBLONG. Then, Obidiah, I wish you to meet a friend of mine. (*Calling*) Michael! Will you come here, please? A shrewd bird Bobblenob and knows the Island. Michael Magpie; Obidiah Bobblenob.

(MAGPIE *descends the ladder*)

MAGPIE. Awk.

OBLONG. Michael, you have heard Obidiah's predicament?

MAGPIE. Awk.

OBLONG. What do you make of it?

MAGPIE. Tricky. How many eggs to make ten quid?

OBIDIAH. Two hundred, seventy-seven.

OBLONG. And then we should have to paint designs on them you see, before to-morrow morning's market.

MAGPIE. Oh *that's* all right—I'm a dab hand with a paint brush.

OBLONG. Really? Mm—it is sad how often talent and delinquency go hand in hand.

MAGPIE. No, the real snag's getting the eggs in the first place . . .

OBLONG. It is indeed . . .

MAGPIE (*suddenly, to Obidiah*) Hen's eggs?

OBIDIAH. Well, how . . . ?

MAGPIE. Not heron's eggs? Seagull's? Pheasant's? Peewit's?

OBIDIAH. Very tasty, when you can get 'em.

MAGPIE. I can get 'em.

OBIDIAH. Can you?

MAGPIE. Course I can.

OBIDIAH. Two hundred 'seventy seven?

MAGPIE. Easy. Couple each. Can't count, most of 'em.

OBLONG. Michael. There can be no question of *stealing* these eggs from your friends. No Obidiah, not even for this.

MAGPIE. For this they'll give 'em, Obby.

OBLONG. Will they really?

MAGPIE. If I ask them.

OBLONG. Well there we are then! Hope, Obidiah! Do you begin to hope?

OBIDIAH. I do sir!

OBLONG. You fetch your materials; we will collect the eggs. (*To Magpie*) When can we begin?

MAGPIE. As soon as the moon comes up.

OBLONG. Oh.

(*The* STORYTELLER *enters*)

Ah. Would you bring the moon up?

(*A white moon ascends; bright moonlight*)

Thank you. Now my friends, to work!

(OBIDIAH *exits in one direction;* OBLONG *and* MAGPIE *in the other*)

STORYTELLER. For half that night they walked the island from one nest to another, and everywhere they met with success. Some birds gave their eggs because they knew Mike Magpie, many because they took a fancy to Sir Oblong, most because they detested Baron Bolligrew and wished to see him foiled. Some gave one, some gave two, some as many as half a dozen, and by one'clock in the morning the collection totalled . . .

(OBIDIAH *enters with painting implements and books of designs;*
OBLONG *and* MAGPIE *with basket of eggs*)

OBLONG. Two hundred and seventy-seven! Michael my dear
Magpie, I have no words to express my admiration for your re-
sourcefulness and the high esteem in which you are evidently held
by these excellent birds.

MAGPIE. Awk!

OBLONG. Now, Obidiah we are in your hands. First I suppose we
must boil them?

OBIDIAH. It's plain to see you don't know much about egg paintin'
sir. First we paints 'em, then we boils 'em; thus preparing the egg
itself for consumption and fixin' the colours used in the design. We
don't speak of boilin' an egg in the trade, we speaks of fixin' an egg.

OBLONG. How interesting.

OBIDIAH. Yes. I have brought along one of my old books of
sample designs.

OBLONG. Very sensible.

(OBLONG *and* MAGPIE *look at the book*)

Mm. These look rather ambitious, Obidiah.

OBIDIAH. These (*producing another book*) are simpler designs for
the use of apprentices.

OBLONG. Ah. Ah, that's more like it.

MAGPIE. Pooh. (*Takes the other book*)

OBLONG. Well then, let's commence.

(*All in unison sit, take one egg, dip their brush and start work*)

STORYTELLER. And so they commenced, each giving of his best
according to his own ability Obidiah Bobblenob produced his usual
quota of highly professional eggs, Mike Magpie produced a small
number of very ingenious eggs and Sir Oblong a large number of
rather elementary eggs, some of which he painted bright blue all
over. But when the moon went down and dawn came up, they had
done.

(*The moon goes down; the light changes, during which* SIR OBLONG
turns the basket about, presenting the painted side of the eggs to the audience)

OBLONG. Done!

OBIDIAH. And I thanks you all from the bottom of my heart.

MAGPIE. I'm tired.

OBIDIAH. Me too.

OBLONG. I'm a bit fatigued myself. However. Now we must
boiler-fix them, I suppose?

(MAGPIE *falls asleep*)

OBIDIAH (*settling himself comfortably*) One thing we never does in the
trade, sir, is pass straight from the paintin' to the fixin'. The hand

is unsteady and the brain excited. Many a panful of eggs I've seen split from top to bottom by some unchancy journeyman for lack of forty winks.

OBLONG (*attracted*) Forty winks? Have we time?

OBIDIAH. Ample time, sir. Market don't open till ten o'clock. If we takes 'em down to my cottage at nine o'clock, say we take 'em straight from the fixin' to the market and—less chance of runnin' into Squire Blackheart, sir.

OBLONG. That's well thought of. (*Lying down*) Though I'm bound to admit I shouldn't mind crossing swords with the fellow. Upon a legitimate occasion. Do you know his father was an under footman?

(*But* OBIDIAH *too, has fallen asleep.* OBLONG *sleeps, his hands clasped on his tummy*)

STORYTELLER. Now Squire Blackheart, owing to his habit of sleeping in his armour, slept little and rose early. On this particular morning, disturbed by a loose rivet, he rose particularly early and went for an early morning walk, with his favourite hound.

(BLACKHEART *enters downstage, preceded by a cut-out hound on wheels. He crosses and is about to exit, when he double-takes sharply, letting go of the hound, which runs off opposite.* BLACKHEART *tiptoes to the sleepers, inspects them, sees the eggs, reacts, looks furtively off* L *and* R, *draws his sword, raises it high in the air, flat side down, and is about to smash the eggs*)

OBLONG (*still recumbent, opening an eye*) Good morning, Squire.

(BLACKHEART *checks.* OBLONG *rises*)

What are you doing?

BLACKHEART. What d'you think I'm doin'?

OBLONG. I think you are about to destroy Obidiah's eggs.

BLACKHEART. Right.

OBLONG. Not, I think, for the first time.

BLACKHEART. Right. (*pushing Oblong*) Out of me way, fatty.

OBLONG (*resisting*) One moment (*clasping his hand behind his back*) Yesterday, Squire, you permitted yourself to insult me. Varlet and Knave, I think it was.

BLACKHEART. That's it; varlet and knave. I remember.

OBLONG. Blackheart, it is my considered opinion that you are a commonplace rogue and a disgrace to your profession.

BLACKHEART. *Eh?*

OBLONG. One moment. (*He puts his hand under Blackheart's nose, and snaps his finger and thumb*)

BLACKHEART. A-aaah!

(BLACKHEART *makes a terrific swipe, which* OBLONG *nimbly jumps over*)

OBLONG. Not a bad stroke, Squire. Now!

(OBLONG *draws his sword. They fight.* BLACKHEART'S *strokes are lethal but ponderous;* OBLONG *fights light-weight style, great dexterity but no knock-out punch. The* STORYTELLER *enters and watches calmly. The whistle of* BLACKHEART'S *blade and the merry clatter of* OBLONG'S *short sword, their gasping breath, are taken up and exaggerated by a loudspeaker,* OBLONG *is borne backwards off stage by* BLACKHEART, *followed by* OBIDIAH. MAGPIE *hides behind the church with the basket as* BLACKHEART *returns*)

BLACKHEART. The eggs! Where are the blazin' eggs?

(OBLONG *enters limping but determined*)

OBLONG. Come along Squire, we haven't finished.

(BLACKHEART *rushes at him.* OBIDIAH *and* MAGPIE *emerge. Avoiding the combatants, they collide and* MAGPIE *falls.* BLACKHEART *kicks him.*

MAGPIE *seizes Blackheart's leg and nips ankle with his beak*)

Michael, let go! One on to one! That's the rule! Let go immediately!

(OBLONG *is borne off again by* BLACKHEART. MAGPIE *and* OBIDIAH *exit on tiptoe with the basket. The noise of battle ceases on a cry from* BLACKHEART *off.* OBLONG *enters, breathless*)

I'm getting, getting past it. One does not realize.

STORYTELLER. Would perhaps (*nodding discreetly to the exit opposite*) discretion be the better part of valour?

OBLONG. Run away (*He seems tempted for a moment*) No. There's life, life in the old dog yet.

(BLACKHEART *enters also limping*)

BLACKHEART. Had enough, have you?

OBLONG. Certainly not. Lay on, and may the best man win!

(OBLONG *and* BLACKHEART *fight again, watched by the* STORYTELLER? *Despite their differing styles, they are well matched, but it is* OBLONG *who is once again borne off. The din of battle recedes. The* STORYTELLER *walks slowly forward. The noise dwindles, goon-fashion, to infinity*)

STORYTELLER. It is sad but true when men fight the fight goes not to the best man but to the best fighter.

(BOLLIGREW *enters in tearing high spirits, and blows a whistle*)

BOLLIGREW. Court! Court's in session! Draw near!

(*The* MEN-AT-ARMS, PEASANTS, *and the* LORD MAYOR *enter as before*)

That's the spirit! Ah, there you are Bobblenob! Good market this morning? Trade brisk?

(OBIDIAH *smiles sadly*)

Ha ha! Just my little joke, you know. (*He sits*) Well now. (*Surprised*) Where's me colleague?

MAN-AT-ARMS (*looking off*) Coming now, my lord.

BOLLIGREW (*calling, cheerfully*) Come on, Blackheart, I'm waitin'!

(OBLONG *enters limping, with adhesive plaster on his forehead*)

BOLLIGREW. Oh, it's you (*Grinning*) Been in an accident, old man?

OBLONG. You might call it that. (*He sits*)

BOLLIGREW (*sotto voce*) Challenged you, did he?

OBLONG (*sotto voce*) He did challenge me, yes.

BOLLIGREW. Mm. Well, you may think you've had a hiding, but he's let you off pretty lightly—compared to some of the thumpings I've see him hand out, eh, Corporal?

MAN-AT-ARMS. Yes, my lord; that gentleman 'e 'ad words with at the point-to-point.

BOLLIGREW. Blood all over the paddock.

(BOLLIGREW *and the* MEN-AT-ARMS *laugh reminiscently*)

(*Irritably*) Wonder where he is?

MAN-AT-ARMS. 'Spect 'e's 'avin' forty winks, sir.

SECOND MAN-AT-ARMS. Always likes forty winks after a scrimmage, does the Squire, sir. Makes him sleepy.

BOLLIGREW. Well I'm not waitin'. Bobblenob, stand forward. Oh, it occurs to me, Oblong, that you and I might disagree on the verdict.

OBLONG. Quite likely.

BOLLIGREW. Well, we don't want poor old Bobblenob held up by the delays of the Court, do we?

OBLONG. No.

BOLLIGREW. No. So I'll appoint another Magistrate. Corporal, you're a Magistrate. Siddown. I've been thinkin' about this case, Corporal, and I'm afraid I can't let it go on any longer. What do you think?

MAN-AT-ARMS. If 'e don't pay up to-day, my lord, I should put 'im inside.

BOLLIGREW. That would be *too* severe. But I'm afraid I shall have to take his cottage, you know.

MAN-AT-ARMS. If 'e don't pay up to-day, my lord, I should take 'is cottage.

BOLLIGREW. That's settled then. Cheer up, Oblong. Bobblenob's probably *got* the money to-day! Got the money, Bobblenob?

OBIDIAH. Yes, my lord.

BOLLIGREW. Well now, look here, this can't go . . . *Eh?* You have?

OBIDIAH. Yes, my lord. Ten pounds; the proceeds of my painted egg stall this morning. (*He holds out the money*)

OBLONG. You seem surprised, Baron?

BOLLIGREW. Surprised? Well I—well—I—we—er . . .

OBLONG. We did have a little trouble getting the eggs.

BOLLIGREW (*staring at him, hypnotized*) The eggs. Yes, you would.

OBLONG. And then of course the mysterious hooligan turned up.

BOLLIGREW. Oh. The 'ooligan . . .

OBLONG. Yes.

BOLLIGREW. You *beat* him?

OBLONG. With some difficulty, but yes, I think I may say I beat him.

BOLLIGREW (*tearing his eyes away from Oblong*) Well, that's very satisfactory! Congratulations, Bobblenob. Glad your troubles are over. (*Taking the money*) Court will rise—

(BOLLIGREW *and the* MAN-AT-ARMS *rise*)

OBLONG. One moment, Baron!

BOLLIGREW (*reluctantly*) Court sit.

(BOLLIGREW *and the* MAN-AT-ARMS *sit*)

OBLONG. Baron, I think we can at last establish the identity of this hooligan.

BOLLIGREW (*mopping his forehead with his handkerchief*) You do?

OBLONG. Yes. He left behind him a piece of tangible evidence. (*He produces the enormous black plume from Blackheart's helmet*) Do you know who's it is?

BOLLIGREW (*shaking his head vigorously*) Never seen it before.

MAN-AT-ARMS. That's Squire Black'eart's, my lord.

BOLLIGREW. Idiot!

OBLONG. Well I knew it was, of course, but I'm glad to have that confirmed by our colleague on the Bench here. People's exhibit One.

BOLLIGREW. Look here, Obby old man, what exactly are you goin' to do with that?

OBLONG. I thought of sending it to the Duke's High Court on the mainland.

BOLLIGREW. High Court, eh?

OBLONG. Yes. No doubt the Squire will explain to them *why* a gentleman in his position should persecute a humble egg painter. (*as one struck*) Unless, of course . . .

BOLLIGREW. Yes?

OBLONG. Unless we were to deal with the case in our own little Court here.

BOLLIGREW. I knew you were the right sort, Obby! Just—just give me that thing and—you can rebuild the church!

OBLONG. I shall do that in any case. I was thinking now of the second part of my mission: the restoration of justice here.

BOLLIGREW. Anythin' you say, old man.

OBLONG. Well, in the first place, I think Blackheart himself should resign from the Bench.

BOLLIGREW. He's resigned.

OBLONG. And then—(*confidentially*)—is the Corporal really suitable? I mean, has he really the legal brain?

BOLLIGREW. Complete fool. He's resigned, too. You've resigned, you numbskull. Get off the Bench!

(*The* MAN-AT-ARMS *rises*)

OBLONG. And now, you see, there are just the two of us again.

BOLLIGREW. And very nice too, Obby. Couldn't be happier. Now let's have that, there's a good chap.

OBLONG. You see, there ought to be a third Magistrate in case, as you very shrewdly pointed out, you and I should disagree.

BOLLIGREW (*licking his lips*) A third Magistrate?

OBLONG. What about the Lord Mayor? (*He offers the plume*)

BOLLIGREW (*checking his hand*) The . . .?

OBLONG. Lord Mayor. (*Withdrawing the plume*) Other side, you see, I don't think we shall be competent to judge this case.

BOLLIGREW (*sinister*) Lord Mayor—do you *want* to be a Magistrate?

LORD MAYOR (*with a nervous giggle*) You see, Sir Oblong, I'm delicately situated.

OBLONG. Baron, persuade him.

BOLLIGREW (*between his teeth*) Lord Mayor, I would take it as a personal favour if you would accept a seat on the Bench!

LORD MAYOR (*with another giggle*) Sir Oblong, may we take it that this morning you met Squire Blackheart in personal combat, and, er, defeated him?

OBLONG. Soundly, Lord Mayor.

LORD MAYOR. Then, Baron, I am happy to accept your invitation.

(*The* LORD MAYOR *sits nervously at the far end of the Bench from Bolligrew.* OBLONG *offers the plume again.* BOLLIGREW *snatches it and glowers*)

BOLLIGREW. Court rise!

(BOLLIGREW *leaps to his feet. The* LORD MAYOR *half rises*)

OBLONG. The case, Baron.

BOLLIGREW. Eh?

OBLONG (*indicating the plume in Bolligrew's hands*) The case.

BOLLIGREW. Court sit.

(BOLLIGREW *sits, heavily*)

OBLONG. To my mind, gentlemen, those ten pounds belong to Obidiah Bobblenob.

BOLLIGREW (*stares incredulously, then*) No!

OBLONG. Lord Mayor, what do you think?

BOLLIGREW (*grimly*) Yes, Lord Mayor, what *do* you think?

(*All heads turn to the* LORD MAYOR. *The* PEASANTS *shuffle forward a step in suspense. The* LORD MAYOR *licks his lips, grips his knees, and avoids Bolligrew's glaring eye*)

LORD MAYOR. I agree with Sir Oblong!

OBLONG (*beaming at him*) Well done, Lord Mayor! Very well done indeed! (*He takes the money from Bolligrew's nerveless hand and gives it to Obidiah*) Case dismissed?

LORD MAYOR (*delighted with himself*) Case dismissed!

OBLONG. That's two to one, Baron.

BOLLIGREW (*snarling*) Case dismissed!

(*Triumphal march music and cheering pours from the loudspeaker;* OBLONG *and the* LORD MAYOR *rise, cheering* PEASANTS *crowd round*)

OBLONG. To the Church!

(OBLONG *leads the way, circuitously round the stage; the* PEASANTS *fall in step behind him. In time to the march, the segments of Church are fitted into place. A bell is placed in tower, at which the cheerful pandemonium on the loudspeaker is augmented by Church bells.* OBLONG *is carried shoulder high and all exit,* OBLONG *bowing and waving graciously to left and right.* BOLLIGREW *is left slumped sullen and motionless on the Bench. Off-stage celebrations dwindle to silence on the loudspeaker.* BLACKHEART *enters, looking nervously left and right. His plume is missing, bits of his armour have come loose and flap from him, his sword is broken short and sharply bent.* BOLLIGREW *turns his head and watches him sourly*)

BLACKHEART. Has he gone?

BOLLIGREW. Ha! Me invincible Champion, battling Black'eart!

BLACKHEART. Now don't take that tone, Bolligrew! (*He limps to the Bench and sits with a clatter. Aggrieved*) Feller's a professional. Don't fight like a gentleman. Jumps about like a bally grass'opper! Can't get a decent swipe at 'im. Look at my armour—me best suit!

BOLLIGREW (*roaring*) And 'oo paid for it, might I ask? 'Oo signed the whackin' great cheque for it? (*He rises and soliloquizes, trembling with self-pity*) Here am I, doing no harm to anybody! Followin' the innocent pursuits of a retired country gentleman! Along comes this interferin' little barrel of a chap from the mainland and what do *you* do? You go swaggerin' off like you always do and come back lookin' like a half-opened sardine tin! (*He sits*) Frankly, Black'eart, I'm disappointed.

BLACKHEART. All right, if you feel so inclined, *you* 'ave a go at 'im. An' I'll lay a five-pun 'note to one of your rotten cigars, you never even touch 'im!

BOLLIGREW. Now, now, Black'eart, it's no good carryin' on like that. We've got to think.

BLACKHEART (*dubiously*) Think?

BOLLIGREW. That's it; because I'll tell you what, Black'eart; this chap's some sort of disguised intellectual.

BLACKHEART. Oh Lor' . . .

BOLLIGREW. Yes, we're in trouble. Because it's no good pretendin' that you and me are brainy blokes, Blackheart. We're not. You especially . . . (*He rises, he thinks*) Got it! (*To the Storyteller*) You: fetch me Secretary.

STORYTELLER. My Lord.

BOLLIGREW. We need help, Blackheart, and I think I know where we can get it.

(A SECRETARY *enters)*

(Rising) Secretary, take a letter.

(The SECRETARY *mimes shorthand while* BOLLIGREW *strolls about, dictating)*

To Doctor Beelzebub Moloch, Dean of the Faculty of Magic and Regius Professor of Wickedness, at the University, Oxford. "My dear Moloch, finding myself in a difficulty, my thoughts turn to the most distinguished living practitioner of the Art of Magic." No, say "the Science of Magic" He'll like that. "The situation is one which I know will engage your disinterested attention, but I need hardly say that expense is no object." No, that's a bit crude—"disinterested attention but I shall of course expect to defray your expenses. Er, perhaps you could spare me a week or two of your valuable time during the next long vac., Yours etc. Bolligrew."

(The STORYTELLER *enters, looking grave)*

STORYTELLER. Baron Bolligrew, there is a letter for you.

BOLLIGREW. Oh?

STORYTELLER. It's from the Dragon.

(All flinch)

BLACKHEART *(rising)* The *Dragon*?

SECRETARY. D-dragon!

BOLLIGREW. How d'you know it's from the Dragon?

STORYTELLER. I know the handwriting, my lord. And—it's in an asbestos envelope.

BOLLIGREW *(licking his lips)* Well, bring it.

(The STORYTELLER *exits)*

BLACKHEART *(uneasy)* Look here, Bolligrew . . .

BOLLIGREW *(excited, though fearful)* No, wait a bit. This may be very handy.

(The STORYTELLER *enters. He carries in a pair of tongs a large grey envelope, which smokes slightly.* BOLLIGREW *takes it, gingerly opens it. A magnesium flash and smoke rises from envelope.* BOLLIGREW *blows on his fingers, extracts a paper, charred at the edges. The others watch as he reads)*

BOLLIGREW. Ah-ha! Eh? What? *(To the Secretary)* You get that letter off to Moloch.

BLACKHEART. What does he say?

BOLLIGREW. He says—he's hungry.

CURTAIN

ACT II

When the CURTAIN *rises, the stage is dark except for the spot in which the* STORYTELLER *stands.*

STORYTELLER. When Doctor Moloch, the Professor of Magic, received the Baron's letter, he was at first reluctant to leave his luxurious rooms in the heart of an ancient University Town for so remote and uncultivated a spot as the Bolligrew Islands. But then he reflected that it would make a change from his usual routine and that the Baron, after all, was rich and could be made to pay.

(*The* LIGHTS *come up.* BOLLIGREW, MOLOCH *and* BLACKHEART *enter.* MOLOCH *is a snappish intellectual; he wears an academic gown*)

BOLLIGREW. Enjoy your meal, I hope, Doctor?

MOLOCH. Passable. Bolligrew, in the first of the month I must be back on the mainland. I am to address an important meeting of the Merlin Society. Let's get down to business.

BOLLIGREW. Right. Well, first there's this Royal Knight Errant, Oblong.

MOLOCH. Yes. You wish him made away with? Turned into a frog —something of that order?

BOLLIGREW. No! If he disappears altogether we shall have trouble from the mainland; Duke; King, maybe.

MOLOCH. Awkward. And then?

BOLLIGREW. Then there's the Dragon.

MOLOCH. Yes. This is an aspect of your matter which I don't much care for, Bolligrew. Tell me again?

BOLLIGREW. Well as you know, we 'ave this agreement. I 'ave this side of the island for grindin' the faces of the poor, and Dragon 'as that side of the Island for ravagin'.'

MOLOCH. And now he says?

BOLLIGREW. Now 'e says e's ravaged it! There's nothin' more to eat there, and he's hungry.

MOLOCH. Hungry. I like it less and less, you know. And in his letter he proposes . . .?

BOLLIGREW. He proposes I should let him have half *my* half! Well I can see as far through a brick wall as the next chap. Thin end of the wedge, that is.

MOLOCH. Mmm! You do realize, Bolligrew, that a spell against a Dragon would be expensive?

BOLLIGREW. Oh yes.

MOLOCH. I mean really very expensive.

BOLLIGREW. Bound to be. Not far short of ten quid, I was thinkin'.

MOLOCH (*amused*) Ten pounds? Twenty-five. Guineas.

BOLLIGREW. All right. Done.

(*They shake hands.* MOLOCH *paces away considering*)

BLACKHEART. Tricky situation, eh?

MOLOCH (*with a patronizing smile*) I dare say we shall think of something, Squire. This Oblong Unselfish? Gentle? High principles? Nice with the kiddies? Kind to animals? In short, a *good* man.

BLACKHEART. Sickenin'. He talks to animals.

MOLOCH. And they understand him?

BOLLIGREW. Seem to.

MOLOCH. Then he's very good. Unless like me he's very bad. Which isn't very likely. Excellent. Dragons like good men.

BLACKHEART. Do they?

MOLOCH. Yes, they have a flavour all of their own. Gentlemen, if the Dragon were to eat Sir Oblong, this would dispose of Sir Oblong, —pretty finally—and I don't think we need anticipate any very fevered reaction from the mainland. For a Knight Errant to be eaten is an occupational risk and common enough.

BLACKHEART. Right!

MOLOCH. If Sir Oblong had previously been treated with some reliable dragon poison—well that would dispose of the Dragon, would it not?

BLACKHEART. I must say, Moloch, when you clever fellers put on your thinkin' caps—it's a treat to listen to yer.

MOLOCH. Thank you Squire. It remains to effect a meeting between the Dragon and our victim.

BOLLIGREW. Yes it does! 'Cause I tell you Moloch, if once that beast sets foot in my half of the island . . .!

MOLOCH. No no, the victim will go to him. Either you as my client, or I as your consultant, will say: "Oblong, at such an hour on such a day, be off to the Dragon's den" and off he will go.

BLACKHEART. Will he? Why?

MOLOCH. Because, my dear Squire, he will be under a spell; another rather expensive spell I'm afraid, Baron, the ingredients are very costly, very rare—snake's feet, fishfeathers, things of that sort—shall we say another twenty-five?

BOLLIGREW. Another twent . . .! That's fifty quid!

MOLOCH. Guineas. Bolligrew, in mine as any other profession, cheap is cheap—and your Dragon is no fool.

BLACKHEART. Somethin' in that you know.

BOLLIGREW (*venomously*) All right. Agreed.

MOLOCH. Very wise. (*To the Storyteller*) I shall need a small basket of apples.

STORYTELLER. I have them here, Doctor. (*He produces a basket of apples from the wings*)

MOLOCH. These will do nicely. And now I need Sir Oblong.

STORYTELLER (*gravely*) Yes Doctor, I know. (*He starts to go, then turns*) Doctor . . .

MOLOCH. Well?

STORYTELLER. Are you sure you want this?

MOLOCH. You are, I think, the Storyteller?

STORYTELLER. Yes.

MOLOCH. Then you know what's going to happen in the story?

STORYTELLER. Yes, that's why I . . .

MOLOCH (*holding up his hand*) You're certain you know what's going to happen.

STORYTELLER. Quite certain.

MOLOCH. That must give you a pleasant feeling of superiority —However, if you're quite certain you know what will happen, whatever is it will happen quite certainly.

STORYTELLER. Yes.

MOLOCH (*shrill*) Then what is the good of asking me if I *want* it to happen? Like everyone else, so far as I'm able, I'll *do* what I want.

STORYTELLER. Just so, Doctor.

MOLOCH. Then, Sir Oblong?

(*The* STORYTELLER *exits*)

The path to Hell is paved with good intentions. It must be very soggy underfoot. (*He turns briskly and calls*) Mazeppa!

(MAZEPPA, *a magpie, carrying a box, books and a wand, enters behind the others*)

BLACKHEART. Eh!

BOLLIGREW. Magpie! (*He raises his gun*)

(MOLOCH *stamps his foot and points an imperious finger. There is a magnesium flash, the gun flies from* BOLLIGREW's *hand, who shakes as if from an electric shock*)

Wh–wh–wh–wa–wa–what the bl–up–lu–blazes . . .

MOLOCH (*indifferently*) Mazeppa my dear, prepare the ground for the mortification of apples while I look up the incantation.

(MAZEPPA *takes some chalk from the box and draws a complex caballistic pattern on floor, while* MOLOCH *consults a book*)

You have had a narrow escape, Bolligrew, Mazeppa is my familiar. The bird is priceless and took years to train. Had you shot him I should probably have lost my temper and done something irreversible to you. Yes, here we are. Is all ready, Mazeppa?

MAZEPPA. Ready, Master.

(MAZEPPA *hands the wand to* MOLOCH, *receiving from him the book from which he reads in a low croaking monotone, circling round the pattern in which the apple is placed*)

Bumbly-wumbly, peejly-weejly. Weejly-peejly bumbly wumbly, etc. . . .

MOLOCH (*over Mazeppa, and much clearer*)

That Oblong with his own last breath
May be the means of Dragon's death,
Lord of Darkness hear the plea
Of Beelzebub Moloch, P.H.D.!

Rosy apple, healthy fruit
Of healthy tree with healthy root,
I call down by magic art
The unqualified canker of the heart.

I summon up my utmost might
'And plant in you the invisible blight.
That he who tastes may wish for more
Taste sweetband sound, AND HAVE NO CORE!

(*A thin column of smoke rises from the apple, as* MOLOCH *applies the wand to it*)

Splendid. Clean up, Mazeppa, and make the usual entry in the journal.

(*The others come cautiously forward and peer warily at the apple*)

It's quite safe gentlemen; what you saw was merely the virtue leaving it. *But*—any person who eats so much as one bite of this apple, becomes instant Dragon poison.

BLACKHEART. Well I call that dashed ingenious.

(MAZEPPA *exits with his props*)

MOLOCH. A simple process, Squire, but effective. Our next task is more difficult. In order to bring Oblong in our power, I need from him some dearly prized possession.

BLACKHEART. Oblong's got no prized possessions.

BOLLIGREW. Yes 'e 'as. That purple mantle!

BLACKHEART (*evidently touched on the raw*) Ah!

MOLOCH. He prizes it?

BLACKHEART (*resentfully*) 'E prizes it all right. Swaggerin' up an' down the 'Igh Street . . .

BOLLIGREW. Never takes it off!

MOLOCH. We must persuade him to.

BLACKHEART (*looking off*) 'E's 'ere.

MOLOCH. I must have that mantle.

(OBLONG *enters*)

OBLONG. Good evening, Baron.

BOLLIGREW. 'Evening, Oblong! What brings you up here?

OBLONG. I have a serious complaint to make.

BOLLIGREW (*listening intently*) Oh?

(BOLLIGREW *signs to Blackheart, who goes behind Oblong and clumsily tries to detach his mantle*)

OBLONG. Obidiah Bobblenob has been placed in the stocks on the village green.

BOLLIGREW. Has he?

OBLONG. He has. And your men at arms are pelting him with treacle pies. Hot, treacle pies.

BOLLIGREW. Are they now?

OBLONG. They have, as I expect you know . . . (*he spins round and draws his sword*) Blackheart, what are you about?

MOLOCH (*hastily coming forward; benign, ecclesiastical*) Is it Oblong *fitz* Oblong?

OBLONG. Er, well, yes.

MOLOCH. Let me take your hand sir. In these degenerate days, a real Knight Errant of the good old school—a privilege. My name is Innocent, Doctor Innocent, Dean of Divinity and unworthy Professor of Goodness at the University.

OBLONG (*respectfully*) Oh. A privilege to meet *you* sir.

MOLOCH. Er—(*he draws Oblong aside*)—you're having a wonderful effect here you know.

OBLONG. Things are a little better than they were I suppose.

MOLOCH. Wonderfully better, wonderfully. And you know— (*very confidential*)—you're beginning to have an effect on our friend here.

OBLONG. Bolligrew?

MOLOCH. I know. But I have been poor Jasper's spiritual adviser many years now—stony ground, Sir Oblong, stony ground—but there's good in the man, oh yes. And *you* have set it in motion, where I failed.

OBLONG. Well I should like to think so.

MOLOCH (*to Bolligrew*) My son . . .

BOLLIGREW. Er, yes, Father?

MOLOCH. I want you to go and release that poor fellow from the stocks.

BOLLIGREW. Oh. Er, very well, Father. (*He starts to go*)

MOLOCH. And humbly beg his pardon.

BOLLIGREW. Eh?

MOLOCH. As an act of repentance. You will feel the better for it, won't he, Sir Oblong? (*He nods vigorously at Bolligrew behind Oblong's back*)

OBLONG. You will, Bolligrew, honestly.

BOLLIGREW. Oh. Well. If *you* say so, Oblong. (*To Blackheart*) Comn' reportin' then?

(BLACKHEART *and* BOLLIGREW *exit*)

OBLONG. I must say that's very gratifying.

MOLOCH. A great gift of yours, this, Sir Oblong. Mightier than the sword I do assure you.

OBLONG. Doctor, you make me ashamed.

MOLOCH. No no, Yours is a noble calling. Ah, this is the famous purple mantle. A prized possession I imagine.

OBLONG. I must confess it is.

MOLOCH. And rightly so. Dear, dear, it's torn.

OBLONG. It's a hurly-burly sort of life, Doctor.

MOLOCH (*trying to take the mantle*) Let me repair it.

OBLONG. Oh no—(*alarmed*)—really . . .

MOLOCH (*desisting; with a silvery chuckle*) The workman is worthy of his hire. I was at one time, Abbot of St Clare's and there our daily task was the repair and manufacture of—oh, church vestments, altar-cloths, exquisite work; I often regret those quiet days with the needle. (*He unfastens Oblong's mantle*) And you will give much pleasure to a foolish old man in the evening of his days;

OBLONG. But I never—(*faltering under Moloch's gentle gaze*) never take it off—really . . .

MOLOCH (*wagging a roguish finger*) Never take it off, Sir Oblong? Do I detect a little vanity at work? A last little flicker of worldly pride?

OBLONG (*relinquishing it*) I shall value it the more for your attention.

MOLOCH. Well! Oh—before I go, sir, let me press you to an apple. I always bring a basket for Jasper. I grow them myself in the college garden. Do tell me what you think. (*He hands Oblong the enchanted apple*)

(OBLONG *bites*)

Good?

OBLONG. It's perfect!

MOLOCH. Well, you if anyone should know perfection—even in an apple.

OBLONG (*delighted, deprecating*) Oh, doctor . . .

MOLOCH. No false modesty I beg. (*He starts to go, then turns*) Let Oblong put his faith in Oblong's goodness, and Oblong is invincible.

(MOLOCH *exits. The* STORYTELLER *enters*)

OBLONG. That excellent old man came just in time!

STORYTELLER. Indeed?

OBLONG. Indeed. I was in danger of adopting violent and even underhand methods on this mission.

STORYTELLER. And now?

OBLONG. Now I shall rely on simple goodness.

STORYTELLER. I see. Is that wise.

OBLONG. Wise? It's right! Oh how much better to have reformed Bolligrew than merely to have conquered him.

STORYTELLER. Have you reformed Bolligrew?

OBLONG. I've made a start. (*Beaming, excited, complacent*) It seems I have a gift for it.

STORYTELLER. And will you reform—the Dragon?

OBLONG. The Dragon! I say that *would* be something—after all, I reformed Michael Magpie.

STORYTELLER. Did you now?

OBLONG. Oh yes—he used to be a thief you know . . .

STORYTELLER. Used to be?

(MAGPIE *enters running. He skids to a halt when he sees them. We see behind his back the twinkling Lord Mayor's Chain*)

MAGPIE. Awk!

OBLONG (*pleased*) Ah—Michael—we were just—(*noticing Magpie's awkwardly innocent posture*) Michael?

MAGPIE. Awk?

OBLONG. What have you got behind your back?

MAGPIE. Behind my back? (*Elaborately he searches the stage behind him, passing the chain from hand to hand to keep it hidden as he turns*)

OBLONG. Michael!

MAGPIE. Awk! (*He shows the chain*)

(*The* STORYTELLER *coughs discreetly, and looks dryly at Oblong*)

STORYTELLER. *Now*, what will you do? (*Quickly*) Think, Sir Oblong.

OBLONG. Think? What is there to think about? Degenerate bird!

MAGPIE. I'm sorry Obby. 'E left it in the garden you see, and the sun was shinin' and it twinkled . . .

OBLONG. That was the temptation. Did you resist? You did not. It twinkled, so you took it—and there we have you in a nutshell.

MAGPIE. Awk.

OBLONG. You may well say so. (*He takes the chain*) I am only thankful Dr Innocent has not witnessed this.

MAGPIE. Awk! Well if you ask me—there's something very fishy about that old geyser . . .

OBLONG. So! Not content with telling untruths, with breaking your word, with thieving—you would now plant in my mind contemptible suspicions against a fine old gentleman who was once the Abbot of St Clare's!

(*The* STORYTELLER *makes gesture of helplessness and exits*)

Michael, it pains me to say this because there is something about you, a certain—gaiety—high spirits—which has won my affection. (*He strokes Magpie*)

MAGPIE (*bending his neck to Oblong's caress; softly*) Awk . . .

OBLONG (*sharply removing his hand*) But that is superficial! You are an unworthy instrument Michael, and until my mission is accomplished, I may not regard you as my friend.

(OBLONG *exits*)

MAGPIE (*stricken*) Awk! Obby. I won't do it again . . .! (*Silence.*

He sniffs) Well *I* don't care. See if I do. (*He hops about stage, jaunty and forlorn, improvising*)

Hi diddledidee,
A Magpie's life for me,
I pinched the Lord Mayor's Chain—
An I 'spect I'll do it again—
I'm happy and I'm free—
A Magpie's life . . .

(*His voice tails unhappily*) Oh dash it! Obby? (*He stumps off, tearful and aggrieved*) It *twinkled*! I *like* twinkly things! *I* can't help it . . .!

(MAGPIE *exits. As he is doing so,* MAZEPPA, MOLOCH, BLACKHEART *and* BOLLIGREW *enter from the opposite side.* MAZEPPA *carries a screen and a box. The* LIGHTS *dim. The air is tense. All keep their voices low. They stop* C, *and all look towards Moloch*)

MOLOCH. Twilight. I can now perform the spell to make one person subject to another. The screen, Mazeppa.

(MAZEPPA *erects the screen and carries the box inside, while* MOLOCH *stands tense and listening*)

BOLLIGREW. Er, Moloch . . .
MOLOCH. Sh . . .!
BOLLIGREW. What?
MOLOCH. I want to hear an owl cry and a church clock strike the hour.

(*Instantly, a distant bell chimes, and an owl shrieks nearby*)

Excellent. (*Moving towards the screen*) Prized possession, Bolligrew.
BOLLIGREW. Moloch, I want to watch this.
MOLOCH. Watch? This is Grimbleboots, probably the most powerful spell in the civilized world—it is certainly the most secret.
BOLLIGREW. I want to watch.
MOLOCH. Out of the question.
BOLLIGREW. In that case, Moloch, I'll ask you for a little demonstration.
MOLOCH. Demonstration?
BOLLIGREW. That's it. Pop this in with the other prized possession, will you? (*He produces Blackheart's black plume from under his jacket, and gives it to Moloch, sweetly*) Just to make sure I'm gettin' me money's worth, you know.
MOLOCH. Bolligrew, I find you offensive.
BOLLIGREW. Aye, most chaps do.

(MOLOCH *goes behind the screen;* BLACKHEART *turns*)

BLACKHEART. 'Ave they started?
BOLLIGREW. Just goin' to.

(*Together they regard the screen*)

BLACKHEART (*wistful*) I envy these brainy blokes, Bolligrew. Must make life deuced interestin'.

(BOLLIGREW *gives an unsympathetic grunt*)

MOLOCH. *Quiet*, please gentleman!

(*There is a short pause. Then, in the dispassionate manner of surgeons, aeroplane pilots or other practised technicians:*)

Retort?
MAZEPPA (*overlapping*) Retort.
MOLOCH. Burner?
MAZEPPA. Burner.
MOLOCH. Essay.

(*A thin column of illuminated pink smoke rises.* MOLOCH *and* MAZEPPA, *overlap as before*)

Trim-spickle-tickle, trim-spickle-tickle, trim-spickle-tickle, trim-spickle-tickle, trim-spickly-wickly! Grimbleboots!
MAZEPPA. Grimbleboots.
MOLOCH. Portent?
MAZEPPA. Portent.
MOLOCH. Presto!

(*There is a soft explosion and a billowing cloud of blue smoke, brightly lit: also twangings and bashings of cymbals and harps on the loudspeaker*)

BLACKHEART. Fascinatin'.
BOLLIGREW. Yes. Needs to be, for fifty quid.
MOLOCH. Prognostication?
MAZEPPA. Possible.
MOLOCH. Proceed.

(*Accompanied by more effects on the loudspeaker, overlapping*)

Scrambled-shambles, pickled-winkles, frightening-lightning eevil-weevil, Knight's a nuisance, Knight's a mess; what he has is his alone and won't be Bolligrew's *unless*—
MAZEPPA. —won't be *Bolligrew's unless*—
BLACKHEART (*nudging Bolligrew*) 'Mentioned you then, old man.
BOLLIGREW. Shut up.
MOLOCH (*with rising excitement*) Shamble's scrambled—
MAZEPPA (*with rising excitement*) Winkle's pickled—
MOLOCH. Lightning frightens—
MAZEPPA. Weevil's evil—
BOTH. By powers of unhappiness!
MAZEPPA (*crying out*) Misery!
MOLOCH (*crying out*) Poverty!
MAZEPPA. Woe!
MOLOCH (*screaming*) Precipitation!

(*Frantic twangings and bashings on the loudspeaker, a geyser of sparks, coloured balls, magnesium streamers, a cloud of smoke.* MOLOCH *emerges with the mantle*)

BLACKHEART. First class show, Doctor. Never seen anythin' like it! Can I 'ave a squint be'ind the scenes?

MOLOCH. By all means, Squire.

(BLACKHEART *goes behind the screen.* MOLOCH *hands the mantle and plume to Bolligrew*)

BOLLIGREW. Don't look any different to me, Moloch.

MOLOCH. I should hope not indeed. The prized possession must be returned to its owner. Only if he accepts it is he in your power.

BOLLIGREW. Oh (*calling*) Blackheart!

BLACKHEART (*emerging*) Terrible smell in there. Yes, old man? Me plume! Where d'you get it?

BOLLIGREW. Oh, feller picked it up somewhere. D'you want it?

BLACKHEART (*taking the plume*) I should say. (*Jamming it into socket of his helmet*) Felt 'alf naked without me plume.

MOLOCH. He is in our power, Squire . . .

BLACKHEART. Yes?

MOLOCH. Sit down!

(BLACKHEART *startled, collapses instantly*)

BLACKHEART (*agreeably*) Like that?

MOLOCH. Get up.

(BLACKHEART *levitates*)

Can you dance?

BLACKHEART. Dance? Lor' no!

MOLOCH. Try.

(*A minuet is heard on the speaker.* BLACKHEART *dances.* BOLLIGREW *is enchanted*)

BOLLIGREW. 'Ere—'ere—let me 'ave a go—Black'eart!

(BLACKHEART *stops*)

BLACKHEART. Yes old man?

(BOLLIGREW *struggles with the wealth of possibility*)

BOLLIGREW (*in a moment of inspiration*) Be a teapot!

(BLACKHEART *stands on one leg, one arm cranked forward as the spout, the other crooked behind him as the handle*)

MOLOCH. Enough, Baron?

BOLLIGREW (*his smile fading*) Not quite, Moloch. Blackheart—(*he points*)—off to the Dragon's den.

BLACKHEART. Dragon's den, old man?

BOLLIGREW. That's right, old man.

BLACKHEART. Oh. All right.

(BLACKHEART *exits, clanking*)

BOLLIGREW. 'Ee's goin'!
MOLOCH. Yes, you'd better stop him.
BOLLIGREW. Blackheart!

(BLACKHEART *enters*)

BLACKHEART. Yes old man?
BOLLIGREW. 'Ang on. (*To Moloch; delighted*) 'E does it all quite willing, don't 'e?
MOLOCH. Oh, the victim does not know he is a victim. A small refinement of my own. Tell him to remove the prized possession.
BOLLIGREW (*to Blackheart*) Take your plume off.

(*A magic effect on the loudspeaker.* BLACKHEART *takes off the plume, shudders and "comes to"*)

BLACKHEART. Well if you ask me, Bolligrew that was in dashed poor taste!
MOLOCH. Mazeppa, take the Squire's plume and burn it. And Mazeppa, kindly make your entry in the journal with more care. The one for this morning is barely legible.
MAZEPPA. Yes, Master.

(MAZEPPA *exits with his props*)

MOLOCH. Now let's see where we are: Oblong has eaten the apple —which makes him dragon poison. You have the prized possession— which gives you power to send him *to* the dragon. It remains to enquire of the Dragon when he would like to dine.
BOLLIGREW. Aye. Right.
BLACKHEART. Er. You goin' to the Dragon's den, old man?
BOLLIGREW. That's right, Black'eart 'an' you're comin' with me.
BLACKHEART. Oh. When?
BOLLIGREW. Now.

(BLACKHEART, MOLOCH and BOLLIGREW *turn their backs on the audience and freeze, as the* LIGHTS *dim further and the* STORYTELLER *enters*)

STORYTELLER. The Dragon lived in a black and silent valley which had once been green with pasture. His den looked like a railway tunnel without any signals or track.

(*A black backdrop descends to cover the church, with a black archway in it*)

Those who had seen him, by moonlight, knew that he was bigger than four carthorses, and sleek, and black, and shiny. Like all black dragons he seldom came out except at night, because his eyes were weak. And in the day, these eyes were all that could be seen of him.

(*Red eyes are switched on in the blackness of the arch*)

And all that could be heard of him was an occasional roar—

(*The* DRAGON *roars on the loudspeaker*)

And an occasional complaint; for the Dragon was always discontented, and talked to himself continually.

DRAGON (*on the loudspeaker throughout his voice is languorous, upper-class, sinister*) I'm bored . . . There's no avoiding it; I'm thoroughly bored . . .

BLACKHEART. Look 'ere, Bolligrew. You see I've just remembered a pressin' engagement.

BOLLIGREW. Well forget it again.

(BOLLIGREW *draws* BLACKHEART *upstage towards the tunnel. The* STORYTELLER *exits*)

Hello? Afternoon! Anyone at 'ome?

DRAGON. Do I hear the voice of a human bean?

(*On the loudspeaker, a noise between that of approaching train and cantering horse; the eyes grow larger*)

BOLLIGREW. It's me! Bolligrew!

(*Clatter of hooves, squeal of brakes. Hiss. Smoke curls from the tunnel roof*)

DRAGON. Oh—Bolligrew! Is that Moloch?

BOLLIGREW. Dragon, we're a bit pressed for time. This proposal of yours for takin' over half of my half of the Island . . .

DRAGON. Yes?

BOLLIGREW. Seems quite reasonable to me.

DRAGON. It does? That's odd! Baron, there are no *strings* attached to this, are there?

(BOLLIGREW *reels out of the Dragon's sight, mopping his brow with his handkerchief*)

BOLLIGREW (*shakily*) Strings, old chap? Don't know what you mean!

DRAGON. Moloch. *You* haven't anything up your smelly old sleeve, have you?

MOLOCH. A reasonable suspicion, Dragon, but the answer happens to be "no". There's something we want you to do.

DRAGON. That's better. What?

BOLLIGREW. Well, it's about this feller Oblong. I don't know if you've heard . . .

DRAGON. I have heard, yes.

BOLLIGREW. Well we were wonderin', if he 'appened to come wanderin' over 'ere, if you might like to, er, well—nosh im!

DRAGON. But Baron, people *don't* wander over here.

MOLOCH. He will dragon, he will. We are using Grimblebook. He will come very quietly—if you wish it, *without* his sword.

DRAGON. Understand. Is he a good man?

MOLOCH. All the way through I think. I shall be interested to hear.

DRAGON. Well. That's worth waiting for.

MOLOCH. To-morrow then, at three o'clock?

DRAGON. To-morrow at three.

BOLLIGREW. There we are then! Good-bye old chap!

DRAGON. Good-bye Baron, good-bye . . .

(*The eye-lights go off. The backcloth flies up to reveal the church.* MOLOCH, BOLLIGREW *and* BLACKHEART *freeze until* OBLONG *enters. The* LIGHTS *come up again*)

MOLOCH. Ah, there you are, sir. We have been all over the Island looking for you. Here's your mended mantle.

OBLONG. Oh thank you. Doctor.

MOLOCH. Turn around sir, and I'll put it on.

(OBLONG *does so, but just before* MOLOCH *can clip it on his back,* OBLONG *moves away and turns*)

OBLONG. I wonder if I should? You're right you know—it's only vanity and worldly pride.

(*Consternation among the conspirators.* MOLOCH *recovers*)

MOLOCH. Come sir, don't be solemn. I spoke in jest!

OBLONG. Oh.

(*The others give an uneasy laugh.* OBLONG *moves back and* MOLOCH *tries again—but once more* OBLONG *moves away*)

MOLOCH (*rather severely*) Many true words spoken in jest, Doctor. I shall begin to think so. Did Gallahad refuse his suit of snow white armour?

BOLLIGREW. Yes.

MOLOCH. No. But Oblong will affect to be unworthy of his purple robe. Here's a vanity indeed.

OBLONG. Oh.

(MOLOCH *and* OBLONG *repeat the same procedure*)

As a gesture of humility, you mean.

MOLOCH. Precisely.

(OBLONG *nods, and is put into the mantle. He is struck by their sudden tension*)

OBLONG. Gentlemen?

BOLLIGREW. 'Ow d'you feel?

OBLONG (*puzzled*) Thank you Baron, the best of health . . .?

MOLOCH (*points*) Oblong. Sit down.

(OBLONG *sits*)

BLACKHEART. Stand up.

(OBLONG *obeys*)

BOLLIGREW. On your knees.

(OBLONG *obeys. They loom over him*)

BOLLIGREW. Well now, you are going to be my guest at the castle for a day.

OBLONG. Oh, thank you.

BOLLIGREW. Don't mention it. At three o'clock to-morrow you are going to the Dragon's den.

OBLONG (*pleasantly*) The Dragon's den?

MOLOCH. Just a social call you know.

BOLLIGREW. So leave your sword outside.

OBLONG. My sword? (*He seems to struggle for a moment*) Whatever you say, Baron.

BOLLIGREW. That's it *exactly*—whatever I say. Stand up. Now cut down to the castle, introduce yourself to the butler, an' e'll show you straight to your dungeon.

OBLONG. Then I'll say *au revoir*.

BOLLIGREW. You say that.

OBLONG. *Au revoir*.

(OBLONG *exits*, BLACKHEART *and* BOLLIGREW *watch him, off, fascinated*)

BLACKHEART. 'E 'asn't a clue, 'as 'e?

BOLLIGREW. Not a blazin' clue! (*Turning*) An' will he go off, just like that, to the Dragon's den?

MOLOCH. At three o'clock to-morrow, just like that; no power on earth can stop him!

(BOLLIGREW, MOLOCH *and* BLACKHEART *exit. The* STORYTELLER *enters*)

STORYTELLER. Now, while all this was happening on the Island, back on the mainland the Duke and his Knights in armour—

(*The* STORYTELLER *breaks off as the* DUKE *and* KNIGHTS *enter, some trundling the Round Table, others, crossing them, pushing off the Church. They all sit at the table and freeze*)

—the Knights in armour were finding that the programme outlined by the Duke, and which they had so much looked forward to, was less enjoyable than they had thought.

DUKE (*heavily*) Anything on the agenda, Juniper?

JUNIPER (*opening the minute book*) The menu for Your Grace's birthday party; er, meringues, raspberry jelly, pickled shrimps, ginger snaps and lemonade.

(*Murmur of boredom and discontent*)

(*Snappishly*) If any of you gentlemen can think of something better . . . !

DUKE. No. No. That will do as well as anything—I suppose. (*Looking round*) Any other business?

TRUMPINGTON. There's a *rumour* going round that there's a dragon—

(*On the word "Dragon" there is a stir of interest all round*)

—down Little Gidding way.

STRONGBODY. I've seen it, gentlemen. 'T's not a dragon. 'T's a big lizard.

(*All slump again*)

SMOOTHE. Anyone know anything about this damsel in distress at East Coker?

(*All stir with interest again*)

FIRST KNIGHT. Went over yesterday, gentlemen. No more distressed than I am.

(*All slump again*)

Deucedly plain girl she was, too . . .

JUNIPER. Well (*He sighs*) that seems to be all, then. (*Shutting the minute book*) Musical bumps?

DUKE. Might as well.

(*Music on the loudspeaker. The* KNIGHTS *and the* DUKE *tramp gloomily round the stage in a circle. Each time the music stops the* KNIGHTS *carefully allow the* DUKE *to seat himself first, then compete among themselves. The* DUKE *calls out the losers*)

Trumpington! Dachwood! Graceless!

(*And so on, until only the* DUKE *and* SMOOTHE *are left. The music stops,* SMOOTHE *assists the* DUKE *to the floor, where he remains, gloomily*)

You're out Smoothe.

(SMOOTHE *returns to the table. There is a flutter of half-hearted applause from the* KNIGHTS)

DUKE. What's the prize?

SMOOTHE (*bringing a box of chocolates from the wings*) Chocolates, your Grace. (*He sits*)

DUKE (*remaining on the floor*) Don't know how it is, gentlemen. Musical bumps—hasn't got the same excitement, somehow. Nor chocolates.

FIRST KNIGHT. Not like it was in Oblong's day.

STRONGBODY. Ah.

TRUMPINGTON. Always plenty goin' on then.

DUKE. One thing after another.

JUNIPER. Best man we ever had.

FIRST KNIGHT. First class.

SMOOTHE (*uncomfortably*) Oh, capital.

DUKE (*from the floor*) That was a dirty trick you played on Oblong, Smoothe.

SMOOTHE. Well, really!

DUKE. You thought of it.

FIRST KNIGHT. Wonder how he's gettin' on there.

STRONGBODY (*enviously*) Up to his neck in it, I bet.

FIRST KNIGHT. Deuced if I don't go and see!

TRUMPINGTON. Make a change.

SMOOTHE. It would.

STRONGBODY. Hanged if I don't come with you!

SMOOTHE. So will I!

TRUMPINGTON. Me too!

JUNIPER. And me!

(*There is an excited babble; all sitting forward. The* DUKE *follows all this jealously then rises*)

DUKE. Gentlemen!

(*Silence*)

An excellent suggestion, but there won't be cabin-space for more than two—and I have had in mind for some time now to pay a State Visit to the Bolligrew Islands.

FIRST KNIGHT (*sotto voce*) Well, really . . . !

SMOOTHE (*smoothly*) I remember Your Grace mentioned that to me the other day.

DUKE (*surprised*) Did I? Yes I believe I did. Smoothe, you can come with me.

SMOOTHE. Very civil of you, sir.

DUKE. I think that's all gentlemen. Meeting adjourned.

FIRST KNIGHT. Well I'll be jiggered.

(*The* KNIGHTS *exit with the Round Table. The* DUKE *addresses the* STORYTELLER)

DUKE. Would you have my galleon got ready please?

STORYTELLER. It's ready now Your Grace.

(*The* CAPTAIN *enters, as before, but now his sail is purple*)

DUKE (*nervously*) If you could arrange for the weather to be better than it usually is . . . ?

STORYTELLER. It's always the same for *that* voyage, Your Grace.

DUKE. No matter. It's not my way to be deflected from the path of duty by a little wind and rain.

STORYTELLER. No Your Grace.

(SMOOTHE *enters with an umbrella. The* DUKE "*boards the galleon*". SMOOTHE *assists. Thunder and lightning crash as the* "*boat*" *moves.* BOLLIGREW *and* BLACKHEART *enter on the opposite side*)

BOLLIGREW. Well Black'eart, to-day's the day—at three o'clock this afternoon our troubles will be ov . . .

(*Thunder and lightning. The* DUKE *is seasick upstage, presenting his posterior,* SMOOTHE *is solicitous*)

'Ello? Must be someone comin'!

(BLACKHEART *scans the* DUKE *through a telescope*)

BLACKHEART. Oh yes. Must be somebody important.

BOLLIGREW. Oh?

BLACKHEART. Purple sails.

BOLLIGREW. Purp . . . ? (*He snatches the telescope*) Ber-lazes! It's the Duke!

BLACKHEART. 'Oo?

BOLLIGREW. The Duke! I'd know that face anywhere.

BLACKHEART. Ah. Duke, eh?

BOLLIGREW. Yes! 'E's comin' to see Oblong!

BLACKHEART (*nodding savagely*) Very likely.

BOLLIGREW. So 'ow can we feed Oblong to the dragon?

BLACKHEART. Oh. We can't then.

BOLLIGREW. That's right, Blackheart we can't. And what's Dragon goin' to do if we don't? I'll tell you what 'e's goin' to do Blackheart—'e's goin' to ravage—indiscriminate! Whackin' great black dragon, ragin' up an' down the 'Igh Street like as not, roarin for 'is nosh—as promised 'im, Blackheart by you an' me—'an that's goin' to take a bit of explainin' too, isn't it?

BLACKHEART. Well what are we goin' to do then?

BOLLIGREW. *I* don't know! (*Mumbling to himself*) What are we goin' to do? (*Roaring at the audience*) What are we—goin'—to— (*Breaking off as he sees the Storyteller*) 'Ere, you, what do we do?

STORYTELLER. You consult Dr Moloch.

BOLLIGREW. Moloch!

BLACKHEART. Moloch!

BOLLIGREW (*calling*) Moloch!

(MOLOCH *enters behind Bolligrew*)

MOLOCH. Yes?

BOLLIGREW. Look.

(MOLOCH *scans the Duke.* SMOOTHE, *the* CAPTAIN *and the* DUKE *exit*)

MOLOCH. Dear, dear. This is an unexpected complication.

BOLLIGREW. Unexpected comp . . . ? It's a blazin' disaster!

MOLOCH. On the contrary, a golden opportunity.

BOLLIGREW. You thought of somethin'?

MOLOCH. I have thought of a way whereby we can send Oblong to the Dragon, and send the Duke away well satisfied with matters here. I should not be surprised if he conferred a Knighthood on the Squire, and on yourself, the order of the golden artichoke.

BOLLIGREW
BLACKHEART } (*advancing; fascinated*) Eh? What? 'Ow?

MOLOCH. You wish a consultation?

BOLLIGREW. 'Ow much?

MOLOCH. My consultation fee is fifteen guineas.

BOLLIGREW. Make it quids.

MOLOCH. Guineas. The Duke will be here in half an hour.

BOLLIGREW. All right—guineas!

MOLOCH. Then listen to my plot . . .

(BOLLIGREW *and* BLACKHEART *come close to Moloch. They all put their heads together and stand conspiratorially, with their backs to the audience*)

STORYTELLER. It was a very wicked plan which Doctor Moloch outlined—

(*They all glance round balefully and suspiciously at the audience, then huddle again*)

—as you shall shortly see.

(*The plotters break up, guffawing*)

MOLOCH. So Baron, if I can handle Oblong, can you handle the Duke?

BOLLIGREW. Leave that to me—I know these bigwigs. Corporal!

(*The* CORPORAL *enters, running*)

CORPORAL. Me lord?

BOLLIGREW. Duke's comin'. Turn out the population. Everyone wearin' 'is best clothes, Corporal—don't want no ostentatious poverty you understand.

CORPORAL. Yes melord.

BOLLIGREW. Issue 'em with shoes, an' everyone to 'ave one packet of paper streamers. Right gettit done. Lord Mayor!

(*The* CORPORAL *exits, running; the* LORD MAYOR *enters, running*)

LORD MAYOR. Baron?

BOLLIGREW. Got those flags we 'ad for the Coronation?

LORD MAYOR. Yes Baron?

BOLLIGREW. Gettem up, Duke's comin'. Cook!

(*The* LORD MAYOR *exits, running; the* COOK *enters, running*)

COOK. My lord?

BOLLIGREW. Duke's comin'. Grade one banquet, twelve o'clock sharp. Orchestra!

(*The* COOK *exits, running; a* DRUMMER *and a* CYMBALIST *enter, running. They meet the Cook with a thud and a crash*)

Duke's comin'. We'll want the National Anthem an' somethin' jolly. Tune up.

(*The* MUSICIANS *tune noisily, augmented by the loudspeaker. The* PEASANTS *enter, carrying shoes. The* CORPORAL *follows*)

CORPORAL. Lef-ri lef-ri lef-ri lef-riii—Alt! Siddown. Put yer shoes on. Other foot stupid!

(*The* LORD MAYOR *enters, backing, calling off*)

LORD MAYOR. Lower away then! Lower away! Thank you!

(*Strings of coloured flags descend*)

CORPORAL. On yer feet!

(*The* PEASANTS *rise, the* CORPORAL *salutes*)

Ready me lord!

MOLOCH. Now then. (*Raising his hand*) Oblong, by the power of Grimbleboots, be here.

(OBLONG *enters, followed unobtrusively by* OBIDIAH *and* MAGPIE)

OBLONG. Good morning, Doctor, Baron. What's all this?
MOLOCH. The Duke has come to see you.
OBLONG. Oh how kind of His Grace!
MOLOCH. Yes. Sir Oblong, when you *meet* the Duke, you are to . . .
OBLONG. I am to what?
MOLOCH. Disgrace yourself.
OBLONG. Disgrace myself? How?
MOLOCH. Well there I thought that you might help me . . .
BOLLIGREW. Pitch a brick through the Lord Mayor's window.
MOLOCH (*hastily*) No no. That's wildly out of character. If you did that His Grace might think that you had been bewitched!
OBLONG (*with a deprecating chuckle*) Good heavens, that would never do!
MOLOCH. No. Have you ever in *fact* done anything disgraceful?
OBLONG. Oh yes.
MOLOCH. Er—you haven't, have you?
OBLONG. I do keep myself on a pretty tight rein, I suppose.
MOLOCH. Aha! I knew you'd have the answer! You have kept yourself on a tight rein now for—what? Fifty years?
OBLONG. Thereabouts.
MOLOCH. High time you let yourself go. Oblong, when you meet the Duke you will simply—let yourself go.
OBLONG. But what shall I do if I let myself go?
MOLOCH. You will do all those things which all those years you have wanted to do and have restrained yourself from doing.
OBLONG (*with a roguish chuckle*) Oh dear . . .
MOLOCH. Yes. Off you go then till you're wanted.

(OBLONG *starts to go, then turns*)

OBLONG. Oh. At three o'clock I have an appointment with the Dragon you know.

MOLOCH. There'll just be nice time. Off with you now. The watchword is: "Let yourself go".

BOLLIGREW
MOLOCH   } (*softly, in unison*) { Let yourself go.
BLACKHEART

OBLONG. Well we *are* going to have an eventful day.

(OBLONG *exits. A* MAN-AT-ARMS *enters*)

MAN-AT-ARMS. Duke's galleon comin' round the 'eadland now me lord!

BOLLIGREW. Right! Duke's comin'! Everybody-y-y—SMILE!

(*The drum and cymbals strike up.* BOLLIGREW *exits in march step, followed by* ALL *except* OBIDIAH, MAGPIE *and the* STORYTELLER)

OBIDIAH. What d'you think of that then?
MAGPIE. What do I think? I think—witchcraft!

(*Boom of cannon and cheering on the loudspeaker*)

STORYTELLER. The cannon fired, the people cheered, and the Duke's private galleon sailed majestically into the harbour. And then for miles around the loyal people of the Island stood smartly to attention as the band struck up—the National Anthem!

("*Colonel Bogey*" *on the loudspeaker.* OBIDIAH *and* STORYTELLER *stand rigid.* MAGPIE *idly scratches himself until called to order by* OBIDIAH, *scandalized. More cheering, then "The Lincolnshire Poacher" and a grand* ENTRANCE *of* PEASANTS, MEN-AT-ARMS, *the* DUKE, BOLLIGREW, *the* BAND, SMOOTHE, BLACKHEART, MOLOCH *and* MAZEPPA. *The* PEASANTS *are prodded by the* MEN-AT-ARMS, *cheering and throwing paper streamers over the* DUKE, *who is enchanted*)

DUKE. Thank you good people! Thank you! Thank you! Well I must say, Bolligrew, I hadn't expected anything like this!

BOLLIGREW. Their own idea Your Grace. I told them Your Grace wouldn't expect any ceremony, but they would turn out. Of course Your Grace is very popular in the Islands.

DUKE. Well that's very nice, very nice. I must say Bolligrew, your people look well cared for.

BOLLIGREW. Now you couldn't 'ave said anythin' which would give me greater pleasure. That's always been my way: anythin' for the people. That's a leaf I took out of Your Grace's book I don't mind admittin'.

DUKE. Well I never. Bolligrew I'm agreeably surprised I'd been given to understand that you were a—well rather a *bad* Baron?

BOLLIGREW (*sadly*) Ah yes. I've 'eard the tales they tell about me on the mainland. That church for instance, I dare say you've been told it was a ruin?

DUKE. I had, yes . . .

BOLLIGREW. Well there it is, there's no stoppin' idle tongues. Blackheart, I wonder where Oblong is?

DUKE. Yes. I take it somewhat amiss, Smoothe, that Oblong isn't here to meet me.

BOLLIGREW. Oh I think we 'ave to make allowances, Your Grace. At 'is time of life we must expect a little neglect of duty. I know Blackheart here has quite a soft spot for the old reprobate, haven't you?

BLACKHEART. Er. Oh. Yes. Yes, rather. Very fond of 'im, I am in a way. Bit of a bully, of course, but . . .

DUKE. Oblong? A bully?

BOLLIGREW. Knocks the peasants about somethin' cruel sometimes.

LORD MAYOR (*pushing forward; timidly desperate*) Your Grace!

BOLLIGREW. Yes Lord Mayor?

(*Two huge* MEN-AT-ARMS *close in on the Lord Mayor*)

Got somethin' to say?

LORD MAYOR. No, my lord.

BOLLIGREW. Oh, sorry. Thought you 'ad. Lord Mayor, Your Grace, just recently appointed 'im a Magistrate. (*Ruefully*) Independent minded little beggar. But I like the people to take part in their own government.

DUKE. Most commendable. But, Oblong . . . ?

BOLLIGREW. He's been goin' to seed pretty rapid since he landed I'm afraid. If it isn't wine-gums it's brandy-snaps. And it takes 'im very nasty.

DUKE. Smoothe! Do you hear this?

SMOOTHE. Yes Your Grace. As Your Grace may remember, I always had my reservations about Oblong.

DUKE. You did, yes, you did.

BOLLIGREW. A good man in 'is day, I believe?

DUKE. The best I ever had!

BOLLIGREW (*nodding*) My friend Doctor Innocent 'ere—'e's a very penetratin' observer of the 'uman scene—he tells me when you're like that, you know, keepin' yourself on a very tight rein, then you're likely to go downhill very rapid if once you *let yourself go*. (*He looks off as he says this. Cheerfully*) And 'ere 'e is! (*His expression changes*) Oh dear, oh dear . . .

(OBLONG *enters, swaggering, and carrying a packet of sweets. All flinch, amazed*)

OBLONG. So! You finally got here! You backsliding old gormandizer.

(*Consternation among all*)

BOLLIGREW. Oh dear, oh dear, 'e's on the winegums again.

MAGPIE (*amazed*) Awk!

OBLONG. Mike Magpie. How you doin', Mike? The only creature on these Islands I would care to call my friend. (*He takes a sweet from the packet*)

BOLLIGREW. The bird is a notorious thief, Your Grace.

(SMOOTHE *utters an exclamation*)

OBLONG. Mike, meet Smoothely—Smoothe. Slippery Smoothe we used to call him. Interesting man. Give you a sound opinion on anything under the sun and sell you his mother for threepence. (*He swaggers to the Duke*) Well, we've put it on a bit, haven't we? (*He chuckles, prodding the Duke's stomach*) How many eclairs have gone into that, I wonder? Whoops-a-daisy! (*He prods again*)

(*The* DUKE *rocks, pop-eyed. There is general consternation*)

SMOOTHE. But this is scandalous! (*He turns*) The National Anthem! Play the National Anthem!

(*"Colonel Bogey" plays again. All rigidly to attention, eyes popping as* OBLONG *and* LORD MAYOR *break gradually into a disgraceful can-can, presenting their posteriors to the Duke, etc. The anthem stops*)

OBLONG (*very excited and breathless*) Ha! (*He snaps his fingers at the Duke, then gathers himself. Daringly*) Knickers!

(*Everyone claps his hands over his ears.* OBLONG *laughs wildly and exits, followed by the* LORD MAYOR. *There is a general babble. The* DUKE *falls fainting into the arms of* SMOOTHE)

SMOOTHE. His Grace! His Grace is Unwell! (*He lowers the Duke to the ground*)

BOLLIGREW. Clear the field! Clear the field!

(*The* PEASANTS *exit, driven by* MEN-AT-ARMS. MAGPIE *and* OBIDIAH, *"hide", behind the Church.* MOLOCH *waves a ginger-beer bottle under the Duke's nose*)

MOLOCH. His Grace revives.

DUKE (*weakly*) Has he gone?

SMOOTHE. Yes, Your Grace.

DUKE (*seizing Bolligrew's wrist*) Oh, Bolligrew, this is the ruin of a noble spirit. Oblong! There never was one like him with a dragon!

BOLLIGREW. Alas, those days 'ave gone.

MOLOCH. Gone indeed. Oblong and our Dragon are on very friendly terms.

DUKE. Friendly . . . ! Smoothe! Can I credit this?

SMOOTHE. It's my experience your Grace that when a man fails in respect, then we may look to him to fail in anything.

DUKE. That's very sound, Smoothe. (*He scrambles up*) And— (*feeling his paunch*)—failed in his respect he most emphatically has! But—Oblong?

BOLLIGREW. Goes over every afternoon to Dragon's den Your Grace. See it for yourself if you wish.

DUKE. The Dragon's den? What for?

MOLOCH. A purely social call so far as one can see.

BOLLIGREW. I sometimes wonder if 'e 'asn't some arrangement with the brute.

MOLOCH. Oh no.

BOLLIGREW. What other explanation is there?

BLACKHEART. Always leaves 'is sword outside.

MOLOCH. That's true, that's true.

DUKE. Gentlemen! You can *show* me this?

BOLLIGREW. This very afternoon Your Grace. I thought we'd 'ave a bite of lunch first: couple of roast oxen, three or four stuffed peacocks, nothin' elaborate.

DUKE. Chestnut stuffing?

BOLLIGREW. Yes, Your Grace.

DUKE. Then, gentlemen, to lunch and after that . . . Oh Oblong! Oblong! To the dragon's den!

(*The* DUKE *exits, followed by* SMOOTHE, BLACKHEART *and* BOLLIGREW. MOLOCH *cautiously watches them away, then turns suddenly*)

MOLOCH. Now Mazeppa, as you see, we approach the climax.

MAZEPPA. Yes, Master.

MOLOCH. I'd be inclined to take a boat at once . . .

MAZEPPA. Master?

MOLOCH. But I haven't yet secured my fee from Bolligrew. Now listen carefully, my dear: go straight down to the harbour, hire a boat, and have it standing by. It's always possible that something may miscarry.

MAZEPPA. Yes, Master.

MOLOCH. Wait here. I'll bring our bags (*going*) I packed them this morning.

(MOLOCH *exits,* MAZEPPA *stands down* C, *looking over the audience in an attitude of waiting.* MAGPIE, *and* OBIDIAH *emerge from behind the Church.*)

MAGPIE. What'd I tell you?

OBIDIAH. Witchcraft.

(MAZEPPA *turns.* OBIDIAH *hides again.* MAZEPPA *and* MAGPIE *confront each other,* MAGPIE *has one hand behind his back*)

MAGPIE. Awk!

MAZEPPA. Awk.

MAGPIE. You're not from these parts, are you?

MAZEPPA. Me? From the Islands? (*Loftily*) I'm from Oxford.

MAGPIE. Go on? You attached to the University, then?

MAZEPPA. Rather depends what you mean. I am personal assistant to Dr Moloch.

MAGPIE (*admiringly*) Moloch the Magician? You must 'ave quite a head-piece on you.

MAZEPPA. I was chosen from a large number of applicants. Yes, I keep our Journal.

MAGPIE. Journal?

MAZEPPA. Journal, yes. A record of all our spells. I often think I could do better without Moloch than Moloch could without me.

MAGPIE. You keep a record of all your spells?

MAZEPPA. Yes.

MAGPIE. You keep it up to date, do you?

MAZEPPA. Oh, yes. Quite up to date.

MAGPIE (*looking off*) Is that Moloch coming now?

(MAZEPPA *looks to see.* MAGPIE *produces a monstrous club from behind his back, and deals* MAZEPPA *a great blow*)

MAZEPPA. Awk!

(MAZEPPA *falls into* MAGPIE's *arms.* OBIDIAH *emerges from the Church*)

OBIDIAH. Eh, Mike, whatever are you doing—?

MAGPIE. No time now—help!

(OBIDIAH *and* MAGPIE *drag* MAZEPPA *behind the Church, just in time for* MAGPIE *to take up Mazeppa's stance as* MOLOCH *enters carrying two cases*)

MOLOCH. There, my dear. That one has my clothes.

(MAGPIE *takes the case*)

This one our equipment.

(MAGPIE *takes the other case, and almost drops it from its weight*)

Careful!

MAGPIE. Blimey!

MOLOCH. Mazeppa, do you feel quite well?

MAGPIE. Dandy! Er-yes, Master.

MOLOCH. Mazeppa, you're not going to have one of your nervous attacks, I hope?

MAGPIE. Awk. Er—no, Master.

MOLOCH. Then off to the Harbour to find a boat. Myself I'm going to get my fee from Bolligrew. At lunch I hope—if not—The Dragon's den.

(MOLOCH *exits.* OBIDIAH *emerges.* MAGPIE *rummages in the case and produces a heavy ledger*)

OBIDIAH. My word—bit of quick thinkin' that was.

MAGPIE (*looking at the ledger*) What's this?

OBIDIAH. Spells K to Z.

MAGPIE. This?

OBIDIAH. Spells A to K.

MAGPIE. Then this must be the Journal!

OBIDIAH. Right! (*He opens it*) Here it is! "Sunday. Performed Spell Grimbleboots. Client: Bolligrew. Victim: Oblong. Purpose: Deliver same to Dragon . . ." The old devil . . . !

MAGPIE. Look up Grimbleboots!

OBIDIAH. What for?

MAGPIE. It'll give the antidote!

OBIDIAH. The antidote! (*Flipping pages*) "Gattlefyg, Gollipog, Grimbleboots!" . . . "Ingredients, Method, Application, Antidote!" (*A pause*) "No antidote exists for this spell . . ." (*He sits*) Baron's done some evil in 'is day. But this beats all. (*Silence*) Pity we can't put 'im under a spell . . .

MAGPIE. We can! Grimbleboots! If Grimbleboots gave Baron power over Oblong, Grimbleboots will give us power over Baron.

OBIDIAH. Stands to reason that does! Mike Magpie—it's you that should've been to that University.

MAGPIE. Ha ha! Ingredients! What are the ingredients?

(OBIDIAH *reads while* MAGPIE *checks tins and bottles*)

OBIDIAH. Snakes' feet.

MAGPIE. Snakes' feet.

OBIDIAH. Baking powder.

MAGPIE. Baking powder.

OBIDIAH. Fish feathers.

MAGPIE. Fish feathers.

OBIDIAH. Table salt.

MAGPIE. No table salt.

OBIDIAH. Got that at 'ome.

MAGPIE. What else?

OBIDIAH. Er—(*his face falls*)—oh deary, deary, me! A prized possession of the victims. Prized possession of Bolligrew's, phew.

MAGPIE. Awk!

OBIDIAH. What?

MAGPIE. You won't tell Obby? (*Backing towards his nest*) It was twinklin' you see. 'E left it on 'is dressin' table and the sun was shining, and the window was open and it twinkled, so—(*He dangles the huge gold watch*) D'you think it'll do?

OBIDIAH. Do? Baron'll go ravin' mad when 'e misses that! That's 'is presentation piece! Well I never thought I'd live to thank a thievish Magpie! Right. Down to my cottage for the table salt. We'll work the spell and then—(*A pause. They look at each other*)—the Dragon's den.

(*The* LIGHTS *dim; the Dragon back-cloth descends as before.* MOLOCH *and* BOLLIGREW *enter hastily*)

BOLLIGREW. Well—(*turning to Moloch*)—if those are the table-manners of a Duke, commend me to the nearest cormorant. Never 'ave I seen a man put back stuffed peacock the way 'e can.

MOLOCH. Bolligrew. I'm in a hurry.

BOLLIGREW. Aye. Right. (*He goes to the mouth of the den*) Hello?

(*The eyes switch on.* BOLLIGREW *flinches*)

Oh, there you are.

DRAGON. Here I am, where is Oblong?

BOLLIGREW. Be comin' any minute.

DRAGON. And you want me to eat him.

BOLLIGREW. Well that's easy enough isn't it?

DRAGON. It is, Bolligrew, yes. That's what makes me, just a little, wonder . . .

BOLLIGREW. Oh you'll be doin' me a good turn old man, don't you worry! All set then?

DRAGON. All set, Bolligrew.

(*The eyes switch off*)

BOLLIGREW (*to Moloch*) Well. I'll go and bring up the Duke. Sorry you 'ave to go . . . (*He starts to go*)

MOLOCH. My fee. Sixty-five guineas.

BOLLIGREW (*piteously*) Moloch—I'm a ruined man!

MOLOCH. Rubbish.

(BOLLIGREW *pulls a bag from his pocket, but cannot part with the money*)

BOLLIGREW. Knock off the shillings.

MOLOCH. No.

BOLLIGREW (*enraged*) 'Ere you are then. (*He thrusts the bag at him*) And bad luck to yer!

MOLOCH. Good-bye. (*He starts to go, then pauses. He weighs the money-bag thoughtfully, opens it and takes out a coin, unwraps gilt foil from it, puts the coin in his mouth and eats it carefully*) I see—chocolate money. Well, Bolligrew, this time you've over-reached yourself! (*He goes to the den mouth*) Dragon!

(*The eyes switch on*)

DRAGON. Yes, Moloch?

MOLOCH. I have just found out that you are the object of a conspiracy!

DRAGON. You amaze me, Moloch. Go on.

MOLOCH. Bolligrew has given Oblong mortified apples.

DRAGON. Oh yes?

MOLOCH. Yes. I assume he got them from the mainland.

DRAGON. *Must* have done, mustn't he? Any more.

MOLOCH. I'm afraid so. When you have eaten Oblong and have fallen dead.

DRAGON. Yes?

MOLOCH. Then Bolligrew and Blackheart with some show of gallantry will come in there and cut the tail off your corpse.

DRAGON. Really. Now why would they do a thing like that?

MOLOCH. The Duke is here.

DRAGON. Understand. Ingenious scheme, Moloch.

MOLOCH. It has a certain squalid cunning I suppose. Myself I will not be a party to it. In your place I should simply claw Oblong to death, and eat the gallant dragon slayers.

DRAGON. Well of course.

MOLOCH. Oh—Bolligrew is bringing up the Duke. I must go.

DRAGON. Moloch.

MOLOCH. Yes.

DRAGON. Very grateful for the information.

MOLOCH. Not at all.

DRAGON. No, no, Moloch. Information must be paid for.

MOLOCH. Oh—(*hesitating*)—perhaps you'll send me a cheque.

DRAGON. Cash, Moloch.

(*There is the sound of coins on the loudspeaker*)

MOLOCH. Come and get it.

(MOLOCH *licks his lips and hovers at the mouth of the den, fascinated and frightened*)

Well, I—er . . .

DRAGON. Let's see; these seem to be ten guinea pieces. One (*clink*) two, (*clink*) three, (*clink*)—come in Doctor, come in—

(MOLOCH, *helplessly drawn into den, disappears from sight. His voice too comes on the loudspeaker*)

four, (*clink*) five, (*clink*) . . .

MOLOCH. It's very dark in here . . .

DRAGON. Can you manage? I'm up here. Six, (*clink*) seven, (*clink*) . . .

(*On the loudspeaker there is a clatter and a little gasp from* MOLOCH)

Mind the bones. That's it. Eight, (*clink*) nine, (*clink*)—and . . .

(*There is a roar from the Dragon and a shriek from* MOLOCH)

MOLOCH. Put me down! Put me down!

DRAGON. Moloch, I don't believe that *Bolligrew* thought up that little scheme.

MOLOCH. Help!

DRAGON. No. I think *you* did.

MOLOCH. Help!

DRAGON. Anyway, I'm hungry.

MOLOCH. Dragon—consider your stomach! I am the Regius Professor of Wickedness at . . .

(*There is a shriek, cut short. Silence, then a dreadful champing noise*)

DRAGON. Yuuugh! Disgusting.

(*The* DUKE, SMOOTHE, BOLLIGREW, BLACKHEART, *the* MEN-AT-ARMS, PEASANTS *and* LORD MAYOR *enter*)

BOLLIGREW. Shan't 'ave long to wait your Grace. Oblong's always 'ere 'bout tea-time. Well Sir Percy—ever seen a den as big as that?

SMOOTHE. It is very big . . .

BOLLIGREW (*to the Duke*) You see why, up till now, no-one's cared to tackle 'im.

DUKE. Up till now?

BOLLIGREW. Yes, I think to-day may be the day. Blackheart's fair spoiling for it.

BLACKHEART. Just say the word, Bolligrew, an' I'll be in there an' 'ave 'is tail off in a jiffy.

BOLLIGREW. Courage of a lion, Your Grace.

(*There is an indignant roar from the* DRAGON. *All flinch. Then* BLACKHEART *shakes his fist and roars back*)

Oh yes, he's workin' up to it. To-day's the day all right.

DUKE. You mustn't let him, Bolligrew! That's not a one-man Dragon.

BOLLIGREW. One-man? Oh—I shall go in with 'im, naturally.

DUKE. Bolligrew!

BOLLIGREW. Matter of *noblesse oblige*, Your Grace. Er, if anything goes wrong, you'll not forget the poor and needy of these islands, will you?

DUKE (*moved*) Good Heavens Bolligrew. I'm overwhelmed. And all this while, Smoothe, Oblong—our official representative, is on familiar terms with the brute!

SMOOTHE (*drily*) Yes, Your Grace. I can hardly believe it.

BOLLIGREW (*pointing*) You'll believe your own eyes I hope?

(ALL *look off*)

DUKE. It is. It's Oblong. Good Heavens—he's *whistling!*

(MAGPIE *and* OBIDIAH *enter behind the others.* OBIDIAH *prominently carries the watch*)

OBIDIAH. Baron Bolligrew!

(ALL *turn on hearing Obidiah's tone*)

BOLLIGREW. Don't bother me n . . . 'Ere! That's me presentation piece! (*He takes the watch*) Where d'you get it?

MAGPIE. Awk . . .

BOLLIGREW (*putting the watch on*) Oh you was it?

(OBLONG *is heard off, whistling "Sir Eglamore" as he approaches.* ALL *turn and, as the whistling grows louder, shuffle back to prepare for Oblong's entrance*)

OBIDIAH (*suddenly*) Baron, cartwheel!

(BOLLIGREW *cartwheels.* ALL *turn to him*)

MAGPIE. Another!
OBIDIAH. Another!
MAGPIE. Twirligig!

(BOLLIGREW *handsprings, then crashes in a sitting position, astounded*)

DUKE. Bolligrew . . . !

(OBLONG *enters, whistling.* ALL *spin round towards him. He makes a brisk semicircle, then sticks his sword in the ground down* C)

OBLONG. Bolligrew! Smoothe. People. (*He walks briskly towards the den drawing a ginger-beer bottle from his belt as he goes*) Have a wine-gum, Tum-tum?
DUKE. Certainly not!
OBLONG. Suit yourself.

(OBLONG *disappears into the den*)

BOLLIGREW. See! Just as I said!
OBIDIAH. Baron, call him back.
BOLLIGREW. Come back!
DUKE. Good Lord!

(OBLONG *reappears*)

OBLONG (*pleasantly*) Yes?
DUKE. Smoothe—Smoothe—what's going on?
OBIDIAH. Your Grace. The Baron 'as Sir Oblong in 'is power. And I 'ave Baron in mine. Baron, tell 'im to remove 'is prized possession.
BOLLIGREW. Remove your prized possession.

(OBLONG *plucks the mantle from his back*)

OBLONG (*coming to himself*) Good heavens—Your Grace? Good Heavens—the Dragon's den—my sword! What's happening here? (*He finds the ginger-beer bottle in his belt, looks at it, realizes what it is and throws it from him with a horrified exclamation*)
DUKE. Oblong is himself again. Old friend. I fear you have been foully practised on.
OBIDIAH. Tell 'is Grace it is so.
BOLLIGREW. It is so.
DUKE. Oh infamous!
OBIDIAH. And tell His Grace that you, not Sir Oblong had an agreement with the Dragon.
BOLLIGREW. I, not Sir Oblong, had an agreement with the Dragon.
LORD MAYOR. And have had this many a year . . . !
BOLLIGREW. And have had this—you shurrup!

OBIDIAH. And tell His Grace you did it with the aid of Dr Moloch calling himself Innocent.

BOLLIGREW. Did it with the aid of Dr Moloch, calling 'imself Innocent, yes.

DUKE (*amazed by his comfortably obedient tone*) And you confess this freely?

BOLLIGREW. Do I blazes confess it freely! This man 'ere's bewitched me somehow. 'Ere . . . ! (*He fumbles to unfasten the watch*)

OBIDIAH. Baron. Hands off!

(BOLLIGREW's *hands fly out at arm's length*)

BOLLIGREW. See! See? (*He turns for all to see him*) An' if I'm not greatly mistook, the 'ole of this is 'ighly illegal!

OBLONG. That's perfectly true. Evidence obtained by witchcraft is no evidence whatever—and rightly so. Obidiah I am deeply displeased. Tell the Baron to remove his watch.

OBIDIAH } (*together, overlapping*)   { But Sir . . .
MAGPIE }   { Don't be daft . . .

OBLONG. Immediately, Obidiah.

OBIDIAH. Then Baron, take it off.

(BOLLIGREW *takes off the watch*)

DUKE. Now Baron, repeat your story.

BOLLIGREW. I will do no such thing! Pack of lies from start to finish!

SMOOTHE. Oblong my dear man, you've destroyed your own case.

OBLONG (*quietly*) I can't help that, Smoothe. I cannot countenance the use of witchcraft.

BOLLIGREW. Well I'm glad to see there's *one* honest man 'ere. Besides me! I tell you what Obby—we've been practised on you an' me! We'll 'ave the law on the lot of 'em. Uncover corruption in very 'igh places I dare say. Black'eart saw it. 'E'll be witness!

OBLONG. Bolligrew, you are a transparent rogue and I have nothing to say to you. (*He sounds bitterly sad*) I hope his Grace will send some worthy gentlemen to take my mission to a successful conclusion.

DUKE. Oblong, what's this?

OBLONG. Your Grace I shall never forget how I misbehaved this morning.

DUKE. But you were made to!

OBLONG (*quietly and sharply*) I was not. I was made to let myself go. I let myself go and (*he turns sadly and picks up the mantle*) I fell prey to Dr Moloch, by my vanity and pride.

DUKE. Oh Oblong, really, that's ridiculous.

OBLONG. Not at all. (*He walks towards the sword, thoughtfully, lovingly, folding and stroking it*) I used to say I was not worthy, if truth were told I thought I was too good. Here's my sword. Well. (*Drapes the mantle over the sword*) I will never carry a sword again.

BOLLIGREW. Eh, now look 'ere Obby . . .

(*Immediately* ALL *join, following and vociferously begging, cajoling, urging Oblong to stay, according to their different natures.* "*Be a sport Obby, don't take it like that*", "*Don't leave us Sir Oblong, you're the first Knight Errant we ever 'ad and we don't wish for none better*", "*Oblong, my dear fellow, this is really very fine drawn stuff; I wish you'd reconsider*", "*Look man, every blessed person here is asking for you*", "*Awk! Obby! Don't go off to the mainland now and leave us 'ere to Bolligrew*", "*Come too Obby, place won't be the same without you*", "*Sir Oblong, please —you are a familiar and well-loved figure in the Islands*", "*Remember 'ow we built the Church sir—what's to become of that?*")

OBLONG (*drowned, so that we can only see his firmly upheld hand, and his head shaking in refusal*) No, no, I thank you, but my mind is made up.

DRAGON. My patience is exhausted!

(*Instant silence.* ALL *turn to face the Dragon*)

I can hear human beans. I can smell human beans. And—I'm— HUNGRY . . . !

(*The* LIGHTS *dim, there is the noise on the loudspeaker of the* DRAGON *approaching—the eyes light up and grow larger*)

ALL. The Dragon! The Dragon is at large!

(ALL *scatter, leaving* OBLONG *isolated. After a moment's hesitation, he snatches his mantle, wraps it round his arm, pulls his sword from the stage and rushes into the den*)

OBLONG. An Oblong! An Oblong!

DUKE (*pointing*) Bolligrew! Redeem yourself!

(*There are loud sounds of conflict on the loudspeaker*)

BOLLIGREW. By Jove! Tally-ho!

(BOLLIGREW *crams some cartridges into his shotgun and follows Oblong*)

DUKE. Smoothe—assist them! Smoothe!

(SMOOTHE *follows rather reluctantly*)

Men-at-Arms!

(*The* MEN-AT-ARMS *cheer and follow*)

Poor and needy!

(*The* PEASANTS *and* LORD MAYOR *cheer and follow. Only* BLACK-HEART *is left*)

(*indignantly and rhetorically*) Squire Blackheart! Are you a gentleman or are you not?

BLACKHEART. No, I blazin' well am not!

(*There is a climax of noise on the loudspeaker: shouts, roars, clashing swords, the banging of the shotgun. Then follows a sudden silence—and afterwards a gush of smoke.* BOLLIGREW *and* OBLONG *emerge with a huge black tail, followed by* ALL *the others, smoke-blackened. The* LIGHTS *come up*)

DUKE. Oblong! Peerless Knight! You have surpassed yourself.

OBLONG. No, no Your Grace! The principal credit belongs to the Baron.

DUKE. The Baron?

BOLLIGREW (*shaking his shotgun; beaming and excited*) Got 'im with both barrels. A left and a right! Pow! Pow! Did'n I, Obby?

OBLONG. He did. The beast was on the wing too. Beautiful shots, Baron!

BOLLIGREW. By Jove, that's what I call sport! You can keep yer pheasants. Eh—these Dragons—can you breed 'em, artificial?

OBLONG. I never heard of it. But there are lots of wild ones.

BOLLIGREW. Where?

OBLONG. Up North. Dragons, Goblins, Lord knows what. Very good sport up North I believe.

BOLLIGREW. Black'eart, get ready to pack.

BLACKHEART. Now look 'ere, Bolligrew . . .

BOLLIGREW. You'll love it, Black'eart! (*Aiming his gun at an imaginary dragon*) Pow! pow! Eh—what's the season?

OBLONG. All the year round.

BOLLIGREW. 'Ear that Black'eart—no closed Season. Well you needn't expect to see me back 'ere for some time, if at all.

(*There is a general stir of delight*)

BOLLIGREW. No, no, I shall be missed, I know that, but me mind's made up.

(*The* STORYTELLER *enters. Rhyming dialogue commences*)

STORYTELLER. Then who will rule your people when you've gone?

BOLLIGREW. Fat lot I care! Pow! Pow! Anyone!

DUKE. That timorous gentleman over there?

LORD MAYOR (*quailing under Bolligrew's appraisal*) I thank your Grace, but I'll stay Lord Mayor.

DUKE. The bare-footed fellow showed some resource.

OBIDIAH. I'll stick to my trade, sir—thanks of course.

STORYTELLER. Excuse me your Grace, but it is getting late.

BOLLIGREW (*putting his arm round Oblong*) There's a perfectly obvious candidate!

STORYTELLER. And I ask you to name him with one voice.

ALL. Oblong fitz Oblong!

STORYTELLER. The people's choice—Sir I salute you in a world of

smiles. First Baron Oblong of the Isles! And that of course concluded
the play . . .

OBLONG. It certainly doesn't. I've something to say.

(*The* STORYTELLER *looks at Oblong, struck by his indignant tone*)

We've killed a Dragon, and mended a quarrel . . .

STORYTELLER. What of it?

OBLONG. What of it sir? The *moral!* (*He steps forward*)

STORYTELLER. I beg your pardon. But please keep it short.

OBLONG. It's simply this: My dears, do-what-you-ought. When
there's something you want, and you can't do without it. There are
various ways of going about it . . .

MAGPIE (*righteously*) And a very good way is to—do—what—
you—*should.*

OBLONG. Exactly.

MAGPIE. But a bit of what you fancy, does yer good!

OBLONG. Michael!

MAGPIE. Awk!

Music plays, as—

the CURTAIN *falls*

SCENERY, PROPS, MUSIC AND SOUND

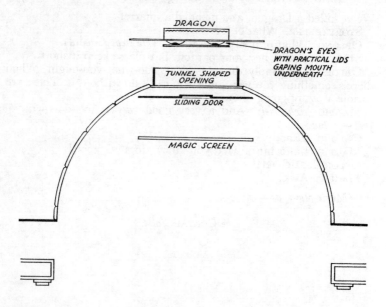

No scenery was used in the London production, apart from the tunnel-shaped opening, just drapes and a cyclorama. The Church was a model and commenced with the "ruin" which consisted of the foundations and the tower, mounted on runners so that it could be dragged about the stage and was able to bear the weight of *Magpie* in the nest which topped it. It was completed by four or five smaller segments constructed to fit into place.

MUSIC and SOUND from speakers in the auditorium were openly artificial and exaggerated.

FURNITURE AND PROPERTY LIST

ACT I

On stage: Round table. *On it:* Charter, agenda
Chairs (number to correspond to Knights) encircling table

Off stage: Dragon's tail (TRUMPINGTON)
Dragon's tail (STRONGBODY)
2 dragon tails (SMOOTHE)
Small dragon's tail (OBLONG)
Brown paper parcel containing purple robe (STORYTELLER)
Mast and sail (CAPTAIN)
Shotgun and cartridges (BOLLIGREW)
Church ruins, comprising base, tower with mace and nest on top, 2 wall pieces, door, blue roof pieces, tower top, bell: wheelbarrow, ladder (STORYTELLER and PEASANTS)
Bench (MEN-AT-ARMS)
Lamp (OBIDIAH)
Painting implements and books (OBIDIAH)
Basket of eggs (OBLONG, MAGPIE)
Cut-out hound (BLACKHEART)
Adhesive plaster (OBLONG)
Money (OBIDIAH)
Broken sword (BLACKHEART)
Notebook and pencil (SECRETARY)
Tongs and smoking letter with flash (STORYTELLER)

Personal: OBLONG: handkerchief, spectacles, paper, pencil, notebook
BOLLIGREW: gold watch, whistle, cigars, lighter
BLACKHEART: monocle, paper

ACT II

Off stage: Basket of trick apples (STORYTELLER)
Box with chalk, books and wand (MAZEPPA)
Lord Mayor's chain (MAGPIE)
Screen and box with smoke and firework effects (MAZEPPA)
Round table and chairs from Act I (KNIGHTS)
Minute book (KNIGHTS)
Box of chocolates (SMOOTHE)
Mast and purple sail (CAPTAIN)
Umbrella (SMOOTHE)
Telescope (BLACKHEART)
Drum and cymbals (MUSICIANS)
Paper streamers (PEASANTS)
Packet of sweets (OBLONG)

Ginger-beer bottle (MOLOCH)
Club (MAGPIE)
2 cases, one containing ledger, tins and bottles (MOLOCH)
Money-bag with chocolate coins (BOLLIGREW)
Ginger-beer bottle (OBLONG)
Black tail (OBLONG)
Personal: BOLLIGREW: handkerchief

LIGHTING PLOT

Property fittings required: nil

An empty stage. The same scene throughout
THE MAIN ACTING AREAS cover the full stage

ACT I

To open:	Black-Out except for single spot down C	
Cue 1	STORYTELLER: ". . . announced like this"	(Page 1)
	Lights up to full	
Cue 2	KNIGHTS exit	(Page 6)
	Black-out except for spot	
Cue 3	OBLONG crosses the stage	(Page 6)
	Lightning flash and lights up to full	
Cue 4	CAPTAIN exits	(Page 7)
	Lightning flash	
Cue 5	OBLONG: ". . . among themselves"	(Page 19)
	Lights dim slowly	
Cue 6	Moon ascends	(Page 22)
	Lights up to bright moonlight effect	
Cue 7	STORYTELLER: ". . . they had done"	(Page 23)
	Lights change to effect of morning	

ACT II

To open:	As opening of Act I	
Cue 8	STORYTELLER: ". . . made to pay"	(Page 31)
	Lights up to full	
Cue 9	MAGPIE exits	(Page 38)
	Lights dim	
Cue 10	STORYTELLER enters	(Page 41)
	Lights dim further	
Cue 11	STORYTELLER: ". . . seen of him"	(Page 42)
	Dragon eyes light up	

Cue 12   DRAGON: ". . . Baron, good-bye"   (Page 43)
        Dragon eyes off; lights up

Cue 13   DUKE "boards the galleon"   (Page 46)
        Lightning

Cue 14   OBIDIAH: ". . . the Dragon's den"   (Page 55)
        Lights dim

Cue 15   BOLLIGREW: "Hello?"   (Page 56)
        Dragon's eyes light up

Cue 16   DRAGON: "All set, Bolligrew"   (Page 56)
        Dragon's eyes off

Cue 17   MOLOCH: "Dragon!"   (Page 56)
        Dragon's eyes light up

Cue 18   DRAGON: "Disgusting"   (Page 58)
        Dragon's eyes off; lights up

Cue 19   DRAGON: "And I'm hungry"   (Page 61)
        Lights dim; Dragon's eyes light up

Cue 20   End of fight   (Page 62)
        Dragon's eyes off

Cue 21   OBLONG and BOLLIGREW enter   (Page 62)
        Lights up to full

EFFECTS PLOT

ACT I

Cue 1   On CURTAIN up   (Page 1)
        Fanfare

Cue 2   TRUMPINGTON sits   (Page 1)
        Fanfare

Cue 3   DUKE: ". . . old Strongbody motto"   (Page 2)
        Fanfare

Cue 4   DUKE: ". . . announcement to make, yes"   (Page 2)
        Fanfare

Cue 5   OBLONG crosses the stage   (Page 6)
        Thunder

Cue 6   CAPTAIN: ". . . go ashore and . . ."   (Page 7)
        Gunshot

Cue 7   CAPTAIN exits   (Page 7)
        Thunder

Cue 8   OBLONG: ". . . the moon yet?"   (Page 22)
        Moon rises

Cue 9   STORYTELLER: ". . . they had done"   (Page 23)
            Moon sinks

Cue 10   BOLLIGREW: "Case dismissed"   (Page 29)
            Triumphal march and cheers

Cue 11   Bell is placed in tower   (Page 29)
            Church bells

Cue 12   General exit   (Page 29)
            Bells and other noise dies away

ACT II

Cue 13   MOLOCH points his finger   (Page 33)
            Magnesium flash

Cue 14   MOLOCH: ". . . strike the hour"   (Page 38)
            Bell chimes and owl shrieks

Cue 15   MOLOCH: "Presto!"   (Page 39)
            Cymbals and harps

Cue 16   MOLOCH: "Precipitation!"   (Page 40)
            Cymbals and harps reach climax then stop

Cue 17   MOLOCH: "Try"   (Page 40)
            Minuet music

Cue 18   BOLLIGREW: "Take your plume off"   (Page 41)
            Magic sound effect

Cue 19   DRAGON: ". . . human bean?"   (Page 42)
            Noise of Dragon approach; smoke

Cue 20   DUKE: "Might as well"   (Page 45)
            Music

Cue 21   At end of game   (Page 45)
            Music stops

Cue 22   DUKE "boards the galleon"   (Page 46)
            Thunder

Cue 23   MAGPIE: "I think—witchcraft!"   (Page 50)
            Cannon fire and cheering

Cue 24   STORYTELLER: ". . . the National Anthem"   (Page 50)
            Colonel Bogey March, followed by The Lincolnshire Poacher

Cue 25   SMOOTHE: ". . . the National Anthem!"   (Page 52)
            Colonel Bogey March

Cue 26   DRAGON: "Cash, Moloch"   (Page 57)
            Clink of coins; continue on cue as indicated through following lines

Cue 27   At climax of fight   (Page 62)
            Gush of smoke

Cue 28   MAGPIE: "Awk!"   (Page 63)
            Music till CURTAIN

37/121